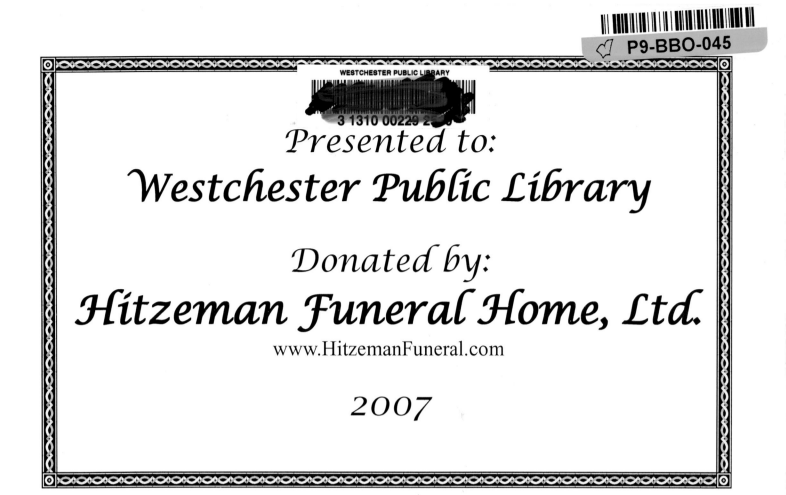

Presented to:

Westchester Public Library

Donated by:

Hitzeman Funeral Home, Ltd.

www.HitzemanFuneral.com

2007

HISTORIC ILLINOIS
An Illustrated History
by Janice Petterchak

Commissioned by the Illinois State Historical Society

Historical Publishing Network
A division of Lammert Incorporated
San Antonio, Texas

First Edition

Copyright © 2005 Historical Publishing Network

ISBN: 1-893619-49-4

Library of Congress Card Catalog Number: 2005930618

Historic Illinois: An Illustrated History

author:	Janice Petterchak
cover artist:	Donald "Putt" Putnam
photo research:	Katy Lammert
contributing writers for "Sharing the Heritage":	Eric Dabney
	Curtis R. Mann
	Edward J. Russo

Historical Publishing Network

president:	Ron Lammert
vice president:	Barry Black
project managers:	Thomas Hankinson
	Joe Neely
	James Loftus
	Robin Neely
	Scot Richmond
director of operations:	Charles A. Newton III
administration:	Angela Lake
	Donna M. Mata
	Judi Free
book sales:	Dee Steidle
production:	Colin Hart
	Michael Reaves
	Craig Mitchell
	John Barr
	Evelyn Hart

PRINTED IN SINGAPORE

CONTENTS

❖

The Rockford, Illinois, waterfront in the twenty-first century.
COURTESY OF THE ROCKFORD AREA CONVENTION & VISITORS BUREAU.

INTRODUCTION

Illinois has been in the forefront of American history—encompassing events and personalities from the distant past into modern times. During the American Revolution, George Rogers Clark captured Fort Kaskaskia to win the western territory from Britain. President Abraham Lincoln, a Springfield attorney, led the country through the excruciating years of the American Civil War. During World War II, University of Chicago scientist Enrico Fermi created a self-sustaining nuclear reaction, for the first time controlling the energy of the atom. And in the 1970s, black Chicago political leader Jesse Jackson became the most visible figure in the national civil rights movement.

Over the decades, Illinoisans influenced the nation in such diverse areas as science, business and labor, politics, social work, literature, and entertainment. Prominent figures include Jane Addams, Black Hawk, John Deere, Marshall Field, Ulysses S. Grant, Ernest Hemingway, John L. Lewis, George Pullman, Ronald Reagan, Adlai Stevenson, Frances Willard, Oprah Winfrey, and Frank Lloyd Wright.

Among the many places commemorating Illinois' rich history are the Springfield-area Lincoln sites, the restored French and British fortifications in southwest Illinois, and Scandinavian and other ethnic sites of Rockford and northern Illinois. Chicago's architectural gems include the water tower and adjacent pumping station—the only downtown buildings to survive the Great Fire of 1871.

Resources for studying Illinois history are found throughout the state, at colleges and universities, public libraries, and historical and genealogical organizations. Since its founding in 1899, the Illinois State Historical Society has been the premier organization for publishing documentary histories, including the multivolume *Collections of the Illinois State Historical Library*, the periodical *Journal of the Illinois State Historical Society*, and a variety of other books and pamphlets.

In researching this **HISTORIC ILLINOIS**, I consulted many of those publications. Newspapers, other periodicals, and websites provided supplementary material, particularly for recent events. Thanks to staff of the Illinois State Historical Library for helping locate information, and to the officers and board members of the Illinois State Historical Society, especially then-President Rand Burnette, Publications Committee chairman and Past President Robert McColley, President-elect David Scott, Director Janet Duitsman Cornelius, and Executive Director William Furry and former Executive Director Tom Teague, for guidance in writing the book.

Janice Petterchak

✧

Clark Raids Fort Sackville by George I. Parrish, Jr. George Rogers Clark led a small detachment of soldiers into Illinois, in 1775, wresting control of many English settlements. His men brought families and established Bellefontaine, the first English-speaking settlement north of the Ohio River. COURTESY OF THE ILLINOIS STATE HISTORICAL SOCIETY.

CHAPTER I

GEOLOGY & PREHISTORY

A state's history may be chronicled by dates, events, scandals and achievements, industrial statistics. But before these must come the people. Where did they come from? How did they adapt to the land? How did they choose to live together?

Some of those choices were predetermined by the forces of nature. Glaciers and rivers created the promise of bountiful harvests in Central Illinois—and left the southern counties a hardscrabble place to live.

- John H. Keiser, *Illinois Vignettes*

In the long ago, even before the Ice Age, the region now known as Illinois—the Land of Lincoln—was covered by tropical waters from the Gulf of Mexico. Eons later, over thousands of years of the Coal Age, the land rose and retreated many times, alternating between sea and forest-covered swampland—each time depositing sand, clay, and shells of marine animals. Later still, after the last of the seas receded, northern ice glaciers advanced into Illinois.

Four times in its geological history—beginning some 250,000 years ago—most of the state was covered by at least one sheet of glacial ice. These massive formations slowly pushed and pulverized deep layers of limestone and other rocks from central and eastern Canada and Minnesota. Each time the temperatures increased, melting ice deposited the rock materials over low-lying regions, forming shallow lakes and wide rivers.

Glaciers of the third period, known as the Illinoian and occurring more than a hundred thousand years ago, reached nearly to the southern tip of the state—further than the earlier Kansan or Nebraskan stages, nearly destroying deposits from those glaciers. The most recent period, the Wisconsinan, covered only the northern and some of the east central areas. Both the Illinoian and Wisconsinan glaciers created the rich and deep soil that is now among the world's most productive agricultural land.

Beneath the surface, multiple layers of minerals are remnants of aged rock and decayed vegetation. The nation's largest deposits of bituminous (soft) coal underlie about two-thirds of the state, with some areas of lead, silica sand, salt brine, limestone, fluorspar, or oil.

The Illinois terrain includes heavy forests and open lands, ranging from flat to gently rolling, even hilly. From the northeast to the southwest lie some wide prairies, bordered with woods along the watercourses. Since the far south, a small western area, and the northwest corner escaped the glaciers, those hilly and scenic lands do not contain the fertile sediment found in the rest of the state.

Between twelve and fifteen thousand years ago, prehistoric humans reached the area that would become Illinois. As many as forty thousand years earlier, their Eurasian ancestors came to the continent over a Bering Sea "land bridge," formed when low sea levels caused ground formations between Siberia and Alaska. This now-submerged land was probably a grassy plain that sustained migratory mammoths.

Over the centuries, bands of the ancient nomads known as Paleo-Indians (10,000 B.C. to 8000 B.C.) moved eastward and southward throughout the Americas. After the final glaciers retreated from near the confluence of the Mississippi and Ohio rivers, those humans briefly roamed the area of Illinois, sheltered in small forest camps or under rock ledges. They survived on mastodon, along with elk, deer, tapir, fish, nuts, berries, and woodland plants. Archeologists have identified unusual grooved projectile points as belonging to those first inhabitants, including finds at several sites in the area of present-day Chicago.

With retreat of the final glacier, the Illinois climate gradually became drier and warmer. Great grasslands evolved, and the mammoth animals disappeared. Paleo descendants intermingled with

❖

The Mississippian people, also known as Moundbuilders, relied heavily on agriculture, especially the cultivation of corn, squash and beans.

COURTESY OF THE ILLINOIS STATE MUSEUM.

new arrivals, adapting to the changing environment. The Archaic-period (8000 B.C. to 500 B.C.) dwellers, less nomadic than their ancestors, developed spear and dart weapons and stone and copper tools, began weaving baskets to gather and store berries and plants, and used mortars and grinding stones to process their food.

One Archaic group camped under a massive sandstone ledge in Randolph County, known today as the Modoc Rock Shelter. In addition to deer, elk, and fish, their sustenance included raccoon and opossum, along with waterfowl and mollusks. Archaeologists believe that the largest number of Modoc dwellers were there between 4000 and 3500 B.C., after which the site probably served as a seasonal hunting camp.

Another Archaic site, seventy miles northeast of present-day St. Louis, Missouri, is Koster, in the Lower Illinois River Valley of Greene County. Beginning about 6500 B.C., people of that culture built circular houses, with stick walls woven around vertical poles. For centuries the Koster people lived peacefully, hunting, fishing, and preserving food in nearby pits. By 2000 B.C., the area surrounding the confluence of the Illinois and Mississippi rivers was one of seven worldwide regions in which the inhabitants independently developed agricultural cultivation.

A millennium later, Woodland-culture Indians (500 B.C. to A.D. 900) evolved to a more settled and complex society. Early Woodlanders produced plant foods, constructed burial mounds, and began making pottery. Middle Woodlanders, also known as Hopewellians, were less primitive than their Early Woodland ancestors. In small villages along streams, they lived in huts made of bark, thatch, and animal skins attached to post and pole frameworks. Middle Woodlanders developed religious beliefs and became weavers and artisans of metals, stones, and shells.

In about the eighth century, Middle Woodlanders designed the bow and arrow, intensifying their hunts for the abundant animal resources. Men provided meat and furs for their families, while the women cultivated plant foods. During autumn and winter, families set up hunting bases in the woods and forests, and in summer moved to the prairie for communal buffalo hunts. Through artifacts found along the Mississippi, archaeologists have determined the existence of trading networks among Middle Woodlanders and peoples from other areas. Some remnants of Middle Woodlander burial mounds are preserved at Albany Mounds, near Rock Island.

Late Woodland tribes primarily hunted and fished, trading their game for other food

and commodities. They crafted pottery that was thinner and more spherical than Middle Woodland designs and made hairpins from bones, hoes and spoons from shells, and pipes and ornaments from stones.

Then from A.D. 900 to 1500, a people known as Mississippian flourished along the Illinois, Mississippi, Ohio, Wabash, and Tennessee rivers. They lived in large fortified villages, their homes made of cane, wood, mud, and thatch. The women produced corn, squash, and beans, while the men were warriors and hunters, devising stone axes and wood-cutting tools. In contrast to the earlier groups, Mississippians were somewhat hierarchical, differentiated by social, religious, economic, and occupational status, and they traded with tribes as far distant as Mexico.

The largest prehistoric site in the country was a Mississippian city near the Mississippi River in southern Illinois. Occupied from A.D. 700 to 1400, the location now known as Cahokia Mounds grew to six square miles, with ten to twenty thousand inhabitants and more than a hundred ceremonial and burial mounds. Today the site is dominated by the largest ancient earthwork in North America, larger even than the Egyptian pyramids—the 100-foot-tall, 14-acre Monks Mound (named

for Trappist monks who came to the area in the early nineteenth century).

During the Late Woodland and Mississippian Periods, some Cahokians migrated northward along the river to Fulton County. Beginning about A.D. 900, they lived in scattered settlements of 10 to 15 acres in an area known as Dickson Mounds. By 1250 the region evolved into a large hunting/farming-based culture of fortified villages and camps, extending several miles upriver.

Vestiges of other Mississippian settlements are evident at Emerald Mound near Lebanon, another extension of the Cahokia community. The Kincaid village in Massac and Pope counties probably served as a trade link between Cahokia and settlements in the Cumberland-Tennessee River valleys.

Then, just prior to the time that Europeans discovered America, the Mississippian culture vanished. A climate change may have made farming more difficult, floods may have destroyed their crops. Wood for fuel and construction may have been depleted, or perhaps disease swept through the settlements. Whatever the cause, when the first foreign explorers arrived in the land that became America, only scattered bands of nomadic hunters remained in Illinois.

✧

The Woodland people were hunters, gatherers and farmers. They used many tools and weapons that were advanced for their time.

COURTESY OF THE ILLINOIS STATE MUSEUM.

ROBERT THOM

CHAPTER II

At first, when we were told of these treeless lands, I imagined that it was a country ravaged by fire, where the soil was so poor that it could produce nothing. But we have certainly observed the contrary; and no better soil can be found, either for corn, for vines, or for any other fruit whatever....

There are prairies three, six, ten, and twenty leagues in length, and three in width, surrounded by forests of the same extent; beyond these, the prairies begin again, so that there is as much of one sort of land as of the other.

- Louis Jolliet, *The Illinois Country*

After prehistoric cultures disappeared, natives of the Iliniwek ("the men") tribe migrated to the fertile grasslands and dense woods that became Illinois. They were members of one of the largest groups of American Indians, the Algonquian-speaking peoples, who occupied much of the eastern half of the continent. The Iliniwek Confederacy comprised Kaskaskia, Cahokia, Tamaroa, Peoria, Michigamea, Moingwena, and several smaller bands. By the mid-1500s, thousands inhabited the state, primarily in the central valley of the Illinois River.

✦

The Treaty of Paris of 1763 ceded Illinois, including the French Fort Chartres, to the British. Painting by Robert Thom.

The Iliniwek (or Illini) lived in mat-covered huts in small villages. Their principal food was maize, cultivated by the women, older men, and children. Other staples included beans, squash, wild fruits, berries, and roots. Twice a year, after spring planting and again in the winter, groups would move sometimes a hundred or more miles to hunt bison and other game. They fashioned the pelts into clothing, made weapons and domestic utensils from the bones, and used various other parts for ornamentation.

The Illini often waged war against their southern neighbors, the Chickasaw and Cherokee, as well as the northern Sioux, sometimes selling the captives into slavery. Then, in about 1570, Iroquois tribes from distant Lake Erie banded into a well-organized confederacy. After destroying or defeating natives in their own area, the Iroquois moved westward. Trading furs for guns and ammunition, by 1655 they invaded the Illinois country. For the next half-century the Iroquois sporadically attacked the Illini, whose retaliatory weapons consisted primarily of bows, arrows, and spears. Gradually, the once-dominant Illini became a weakened and beleaguered confederacy.

Sauk and Fox Tribes, driven from lower Michigan by the Iroquois, replaced the Illini in the northwest section of the state, while northern bands of Potawatomi, Ottawa, and Chippewa moved to an area near Lake Michigan. Kickapoo, also from Michigan, migrated to the central prairies, and Shawnee crossed the Ohio River into the southeast, all engaging in fur trade with newly arriving Europeans. In addition, the Shawnee began mining salt in areas near the Ohio.

French exploration and settlement of Illinois began in earnest in 1673. In May, French-born Jesuit missionary Jacques Marquette, accompanied by five *voyageurs* and young Canadian explorer and mapmaker Louis Jolliet, traveled southward to the Mississippi from the mission of St. Ignace, on the upper Michigan peninsula.

After passing the mouth of the Ohio River and determining that the great Mississippi emptied into the Gulf of Mexico, Marquette and Jolliet returned upstream. Paddling northeast on the Illinois River, they stopped at the native Grand Village of the Illinois, near present-day Utica, then proceeded to the swampy portage at the base of Lake Michigan. There the explorers envisioned a canal that would connect the Great Lakes with the Mississippi River systems. In the spring of 1675 Marquette revisited the Grand Village, founding the Mission of the Immaculate Conception of the

Blessed Virgin. On Easter Sunday he preached conversion to some fifteen hundred natives.

Five years elapsed before another French explorer, René-Robert Cavelier, Sieur de La Salle, led fourteen men into Illinois, including Italian adventurer Henri de Tonti and three Franciscan monks. They planned to establish trading posts and settlements in the Illinois and Mississippi valleys.

Following the Illinois River downstream to Lake Peoria, LaSalle erected crude Fort Crevecoeur, the first French outpost in the west. In 1682 he and Tonti journeyed to the mouth of the Mississippi, and within sight of the Gulf of Mexico claimed the river, its tributaries, and the vast Mississippi valley in the name of Louis XIV, king of France.

Returning to Illinois, LaSalle later built Fort St. Louis on a high bluff across the river from the Grand Village. The fort served as his headquarters, with a surrounding palisade for protection of adjacent dwellings and storehouses. In clusters of nearby towns, perhaps as many as twenty thousand natives of various bands gathered in mutual defense against the Iroquois.

Within a few years the timber and wildlife resources near Fort St. Louis could no longer support the large Indian population, causing La Salle's successor Tonti to abandon the site. In the winter of 1691-92 he accompanied a band of Kaskaskia some eighty miles

downstream and erected a trading post and a larger Fort St. Louis, or Fort Pimitoui, above Lake Peoria. Jesuit priest Jacques Gravier built a chapel near the fort, and Canadian and French followers formed a small village. For the next several years, despite continuing Iroquois threats, trade in the area prospered.

In the northeast part of the Illinois country, Jesuit priest Pierre François Pinet in 1696 established the Mission of the Guardian Angel at the point where the Chicago River flows into Lake Michigan—site of the future city of Chicago. Within only a few years, however, a Fox band, enemies of the Illini as well as the French, forced the priest and natives to abandon the site. Then for nearly a century, until after the American Revolution, no other Europeans would inhabit that area.

To the south, in 1699, three priests from the Quebec Seminary of Foreign Missions founded the Mission of the Holy Family at the Tamaroa village of Cahokia, in the fertile Mississippi River floodplain that would become known as the American Bottom.

The following year the Kaskaskia left Fort Pimitoui, moving southward with French traders and Jesuit missionaries. At a site they named Kaskaskia, near the confluence of the Mississippi and Kaskaskia rivers, priests established the Immaculate Conception mission. For more than a century Kaskaskia would serve as the region's principal commercial outlet, supplying grain to French military posts along the Mississippi and Ohio rivers.

As their territorial civil and military headquarters, the French built Fort de Chartres on a river bluff between the villages of Kaskaskia and Cahokia. Near the fort, French-Canadian colonists established the village of Prairie du Rocher (prairie by the rock), served by the Seminary priests from Cahokia. Cahokia developed as the first permanent settlement and center of French life in the Illinois country. The inhabitants constructed distinctive French-style homes of upright, square-hewn logs, with steeply pitched roofs extending over open porches.

Until 1717 the territory of Illinois was considered a dependency of Canada. Then, as part of the French colony of Louisiana, the area attracted interest from European investors. Scot adventurer John Law convinced the French government to grant his new commercial enterprise, the Company of the West, a twenty-five-year trade monopoly in the Mississippi Valley. Financed by speculator investors, Law received permission to construct forts and settlements and fund lead and salt mining expeditions in the American Bottom. For a few years the Louisiana colony, and with it the Illinois country, became a favored European investment. Eventually, however, poor financial returns and the ongoing threat of Indian attacks burst Law's "Mississippi Bubble," leaving many of his investors bankrupt.

In 1719 French banker Philippe François Renault introduced black slavery in the Illinois country, bringing several hundred Caribbeans for a lead mine operation near Fort de Chartres. Each year he imported additional slaves as mine laborers. Then in 1744, Renault abandoned the business, selling the slaves to French families in the area.

To the north in the Illinois country, Fox bands continued their attacks on Illini villages. In 1722 the Fox forced remaining natives from Fort St. Louis and four years later killed several French soldiers on the Missouri River. The incursions continued until 1730 when, between the Illinois and Wabash rivers, the Fox engaged in a fierce battle with Illini bands and French troops. The Fox were

nearly annihilated, with some three hundred warriors killed or captured, thus ending their threat to the area.

Throughout the first half of the eighteenth century, settlers and traders shipped their mineral and agricultural products of Illinois northward to Detroit, eastward to Ohio River ports, or southward to New Orleans, for transport to the West Indies and Europe. "This country" of colonial Illinois, wrote a

✧

The famed explorer Robert Cavelier, Sieur de La Salle, established trading posts and settlements in Illinois in 1680 before traveling south to the mouth of the Mississippi River, claiming all the tributaries of the great river for Louis XIV, king of France.

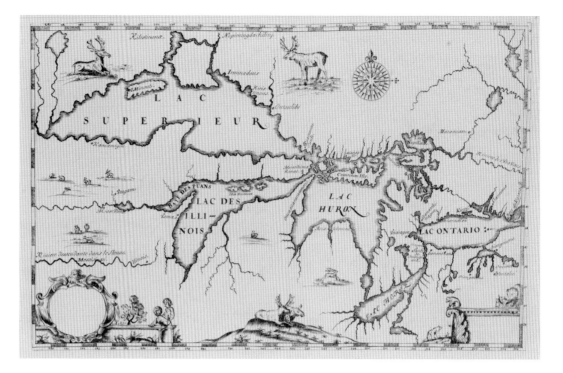

French visitor in 1753, "supplies flour to the southern part of the colony and deals in fur, lead, and salt. Buffalo and deer are particularly fond of the grazing lands surrounding the great number of salt licks in the area. The salted meat and tongues of these animals are sold to New Orleans, the hams are every bit as good as those of Bayonne. The local fruit is as good as that grown in France." In exchange for their products, returning traders supplied settlers with sugar, chocolate, brandy, rice, cotton, yard goods, clothing, and tobacco.

By mid-century, war between France and Great Britain was spreading to their colonial possessions, affecting the Illinois country. As defense against the British and their Iroquois allies, French officials ordered a more formidable fortification at Fort de Chartres. Although never completed, the new structure was considered the strongest outpost in North America, with eighteen-foot walls and quarters for four hundred men.

In 1754 the French-British hostilities escalated in the Ohio River Valley. Early in the French and Indian War, known in Europe as the Seven Years' War, French troops won most of the battles. To strengthen their defenses, in 1757 they constructed Fort Massac along the Ohio River near present-day Metropolis, and Fort Kaskaskia on the Mississippi. Within a

year, however, British soldiers began capturing French villages and forts and eventually won the colonial conflict. By the 1763 Treaty of Paris, France surrendered Canada and the American Midwest, including all of Illinois.

Before British officials arrived in Illinois, however, an Indian chief named Pontiac led a confederacy of Ottawa, Chippewa, Potawatomi, and other tribes against British troops. In May 1763 the natives overran ten of fourteen forts, but British forces soon reestablished garrisons and quelled the rebellion. According to tradition, the tribes later avenged Pontiac's death, presumably by a Peoria warrior, when they stranded and starved an Illini band on the high bluff of Fort St. Louis. From that legend the site became known as Starved Rock.

With British control of the Illinois country, many of the French fur traders relocated across the Mississippi to newly founded St. Louis. The British military and administrative headquarters were initially established at Fort de Chartres, but soon relocated to Kaskaskia, in a fortified building that had once housed the Jesuit missionaries.

Because of the expense and difficulty of administering the distant Illinois country, along with plans to expand fur trade with native tribes, King George III of England decreed a prohibition on settlement west of the Appalachian Mountains. But the westward movement was unstoppable, as eastern trappers and traders, along with farmers and their families, made their way to Illinois. Even before the close of the war, eastern and British merchants began selling wares on banks of the Mississippi and Illinois rivers.

One such enterprise was Baynton, Wharton, and Morgan of Philadelphia. Establishing their main store at Kaskaskia, with a later branch at Cahokia, the partners sold clothing, household utensils, musical instruments, wines, and munitions in exchange for furs and hides. George Morgan, in charge of the Illinois business, brought several hundred Jamaican slaves for sale at the Kaskaskia store. Within a few years, however, the merchants withdrew from Illinois—having found that Canadian firms were better organized in the fur trade and that transporting goods from Pennsylvania by wagon or boat proved more expensive than bringing them upriver from New Orleans.

When the American Revolution began in 1775, British troops in Illinois were ordered to Detroit. A twenty-six-year-old Virginian, Major George Rogers Clark, conceived a plan to drive the enemy from North America; his first goal was to secure the Illinois forts. With approval from Virginia Governor Patrick Henry, Clark and his troops traveled down the Ohio River to Fort Massac, overland through Illinois, and on the evening of July 4, 1778, quietly captured Fort Kaskaskia. The settlers, when told that France had entered the war as an American ally, quickly agreed to assist his soldiers. Within days and without bloodshed, Clark gained control of the American Bottom settlements.

From Kaskaskia, Clark sent a small detachment to British-held Vincennes, on the east bank of the Wabash River, where the soldiers captured and occupied Fort Sackville. But the British lieutenant governor of Detroit, Henry Hamilton, led troops and several hundred Indians downriver, recapturing the fort late in the year. Learning that in spring Hamilton intended to destroy all American settlements west of the Appalachians, Clark planned an immediate assault on Sackville. In

February 1779, he and about 170 men, including French volunteers, began a dangerous eighteen-day march eastward across Illinois, braving brutal winter weather and wading through icy river waters. Reaching Vincennes, they fired into Fort Sackville, and after two days Hamilton and his besieged troops surrendered. With the British ceding all possessions in the Mississippi Valley, the Illinois country was established as an American county of Virginia.

Some members of Clark's army, many from Kentucky and Tennessee, settled with their families along a spring between Cahokia and Prairie du Rocher, near present-day Waterloo. The new town, Bellefontaine, was the first permanent settlement of English-speaking Americans north of the Ohio River.

About that time in northeastern Illinois, a black fur trader and farmer, Jean Baptiste Point du Sable, established a trading post on the north bank of the Chicago River near Lake Michigan. Probably a native of Santo Domingo (now Haiti), du Sable resided at the site with his Potawatomi wife for nearly twenty years, providing flour, bread, and pork to fur traders, British and French travelers, and the area's few settlers.

By the 1783 Treaty of Paris ending the War of Independence, Britain relinquished to American jurisdiction all lands north of the Ohio and east of the Mississippi rivers. The following year Virginia ceded to the federal government its claim to the Illinois country.

Jean Baptiste Point De Saible

✧

Above: Haitian-born settler Jean Baptiste Point du Sable is credited as the founder of Chicago. Chicago's first marriage ceremony, first election, and first court were held in his five-bedroom house, which was the first permanent structure in the area. He was recognized in 1968 as being the "Father of Chicago, Illinois."
COURTESY OF THE CHICAGO HISTORICAL SOCIETY. ENGRAVER - CHARLES C. DAWSON. ENGRAVING; ICHI-27363.

Below: A twentieth-century sketch shows the "Checagou River," with Lake Michigan in the background, at the time of Jean Baptiste Point du Sable.
COURTESY OF THE CHICAGO HISTORICAL SOCIETY. ICHI-34397.

CHAPTER III

To the prairies came men of the north, men of the south, men from Great Britain, Ireland, and Germany; as they built their cabins side by side, and in the same manner as they gave assistance to each other in raising their dwelling houses, they worked shoulder to shoulder in building the structure of the American state which is called Illinois.

- Clarence Walworth Alvord
The Illinois Country, 1673-1818

Following the American Revolution, Congress in 1785 passed legislation known as the Land Ordinance, opening for public sale huge areas, including the future states of Illinois, Ohio, Indiana, Michigan, Wisconsin, and part of Minnesota. The Northwest Ordinance, enacted two years later, established a government for the Northwest Territory, and Arthur St. Clair, a Scots-born war general, was named the first governor and commander of troops.

Framers of the Northwest Ordinance prohibited both slavery and involuntary servitude in the entire Territory. Slave owners in the Illinois country, however, claimed that a provision in the 1784 Virginia cession permitted the retention of slaves obtained prior to the Ordinance. Appeasing those settlers, St. Clair declared that the prohibition did not include slaves already held within the Territory.

Prior to assuming his new command, St. Clair negotiated two treaties with Native Americans to secure land titles in the Territory. In 1790 he arrived in Kaskaskia to establish courts and civil regulations. He gave his own name to the first Illinois county, which included all settlements between the Wabash and the Mississippi rivers.

"The province of Illinois," wrote visiting French official Victor Collot in 1796, "is superior to any description which has been made, for local beauty, fertility, climate, and the means of every kind which nature has lavished upon it for the facility of commerce. This country is a delightful valley, where winds one of the most majestic rivers on the globe, and which, after receiving the vast Missouri, is still augmented by an infinite number of smaller rivers and creeks, all navigable, and fitted for the construction of mills and machinery of almost all kind."

Hostile natives, however, continued disputing the claims of white settlers in the area. In 1791, General St. Clair, leading a poorly equipped force against Ohio tribesmen near Fort Wayne, suffered one of the American army's most crushing defeats. Warfare continued until 1795, when the Treaty of Greenville specified property rights for white settlers but conceded to the natives those areas not occupied by whites or the military. The tribes, in turn, ceded claim to land at every important post and portage, including Fort Massac and the future site of Fort Dearborn, at the mouth of the Chicago River, along with tracts at Peoria and the mouth of the Illinois River.

In 1800, the United States Congress formed the Territory of Indiana, which included Illinois. Vincennes became the capital, and President John Adams appointed General William Henry Harrison as governor and the superintendent of Indian affairs. The population of the Illinois country was 2,458, approximately the same as a half-century earlier.

With Illinois now part of the United States, many of the influential French inhabitants moved across the Mississippi to primarily Catholic, Spanish-held St. Louis. Although the French who remained in Illinois retained their Catholicism, only a few priests resided in the American Bottom and church buildings fell into decay. Protestant ministers made occasional visits, and in 1796 a Baptist preacher established a church south of Bellefontaine at New Design, a village of Virginians who abhorred the use of slave labor.

❖

A painting of Fort Dearborn and the Kinzie House by Edgar S. Cameron, 1911.
COURTESY OF THE CHICAGO HISTORICAL SOCIETY. GLASS NEGATIVE, DN-0009351.

Methodists also began arriving in the area, and in 1803 Reverend Benjamin Young organized a group of circuit riders, leading to a network of Methodist churches in the small communities. Both denominations held annual revivals to attract new members, although most of the settlers affiliated with no church or religion.

Fort Massac, which had been rebuilt in 1794 and garrisoned until 1814, was also the center for trade on the Ohio, Tennessee, and Cumberland rivers. To guard the mouth of the Chicago River in northeastern Illinois, the federal government in 1803 constructed Fort Dearborn on the south bank near Lake Michigan and two years later located an Indian agency and a trading house at Chicago. Trader John Kinzie, who purchased the du Sable post in 1804, is considered Chicago's first white settler.

Yet, primarily because of Governor St. Clair's inability to obtain additional Native American land cessions, potential inhabitants were reluctant to settle in the territory. Then General Harrison, as Indian superintendent, negotiated with individual bands. In an 1803 treaty, he negated the Kaskaskia claim to southern Illinois. In 1804 he persuaded a few Sauk and Fox chiefs to cede some fifty million acres west of the Illinois and Fox rivers, and the following year negotiated with the Miami, an Illini band, for land on the Wabash. By 1809 he obtained treaties surrendering practically all of Ohio, eastern Michigan, southern Indiana, and most of western and southern Illinois.

That year Congress organized the Illinois Territory, which included nearly all of present-day Wisconsin, most of upper Michigan, and eastern Minnesota. The new government maintained an 1803 Indiana territorial law permitting long-term indenture—virtually indistinguishable from slavery. The slavery prohibition specified in the Northwest Ordinance, however, restrained the spread of indentured servitude.

Kaskaskia was selected as the capital for the vast Illinois Territory, and President James Madison appointed Kentucky Supreme Court Chief Justice Ninian Edwards as governor. Awarded a thousand-acre plot of land, Edwards

and his slaves settled in the American Bottom between Kaskaskia and Prairie du Rocher. He held additional duties as commander of the militia, superintendent of Indian affairs, and superintendent of the government-owned salines near Shawneetown—the frontier's primary salt source for treating and preserving meat. In addition, Edwards and his sons became prosperous merchants, establishing stores in southern Illinois and Missouri towns.

Shawneetown developed as a trading post and Ohio River port. One traveler reported that in 1809 the town had "more appearance of business than I have seen this side of Pittsburgh." Still, settlement of interior southern Illinois lands remained slow. The hard, unwooded prairie offered neither material for construction, fuel, or fencing, nor rivers for transporting agrarian goods. Most early settlements, therefore, were along river banks and in the timbered lands—those pioneers arriving by way of the Ohio, Wabash, Mississippi, and Illinois rivers.

An 1800 federal law that allowed land purchases on a four-year credit system helped stimulate migration. When settlers began requesting the right to elect their public officials, Congress in 1812 granted voting rights to free adult males who had resided in Illinois for one year and who paid county or territorial tax. Shadrach Bond, a prominent land official and farmer at New Design, was elected the Illinois Territory's first delegate to Congress.

Meanwhile, increasing Indian resistance to American expansion, organized by the war chief Tecumseh and his brother the Prophet, coincided with British interference with neutral American trade. When the U.S. declared war against Britain in 1812, Tecumseh and his confederacy sided with the British, blockading American ports and raiding American settlements. As the violence increased, Congress assigned companies of mounted rangers to Illinois. Governor Edwards constructed Fort Russell as defense for the new settlement of Edwardsville, with 350 rangers and volunteers, and rebuilt Fort Clark at Peoria. The seventy soldiers at Fort Dearborn and some forty nearby settlers were alerted to impending danger.

In summer of 1812, officers at Fort Dearborn received orders for evacuation to Fort Wayne. About three miles south of the fort, however, some five hundred Indians began firing on the fleeing soldiers and settlers. Only a few Americans escaped, including John Kinzie and his family. Of the nearly sixty who died, some were tortured and executed after they surrendered. The following day, a Potawatomi raiding party burned the fort. In retaliation, that autumn, Governor Edwards led a small army into central Illinois, destroying a Kickapoo village and killing twenty-four warriors.

The westernmost campaign of the War of 1812 occurred two summers later on a Mississippi River island near present-day Rock Island. There a Sauk band and a few British troops defeated federal regulars and Illinois rangers, with the loss of sixteen American lives. The Treaty of Ghent, signed by American and British peace commissioners in December 1814, brought the war to an indecisive end. The final major military action occurred in January, when Major General Andrew Jackson's troops routed British forces at the battle of New Orleans. Several Indian nations lost millions of acres as a result of the three-year war.

Edwards was appointed one of three commissioners to negotiate Indian treaties on the Indiana, Illinois, and Missouri frontiers. They prevailed upon the tribesmen to relinquish title to more than eight million acres. The Potawatomi, Ottawa, and Chippewa gave up claims to land south of Lake Michigan along the Des Plaines, Kankakee, Fox, and Illinois rivers. The tribes continued holding some areas, but the way was now cleared for settlement of all of Illinois.

The U.S. Army rebuilt Fort Dearborn, maintaining its garrison until 1836, by which time the frontier had moved far to the west and northwest. The safety of trading posts throughout the Illinois Territory was increased with restored forts and additional posts at Rock Island (Fort Armstrong) and Peoria (Fort Clark).

After the war, government land offices at the Kaskaskia capital and at the commercial centers of Shawneetown and Edwardsville served pioneers now flooding in from the east and south. The territory's first financial institution, the Bank of Illinois, was established at Shawneetown, with another located in Edwardsville.

The first newspaper, the *Illinois Herald*, was printed in Kaskaskia in 1814, followed in 1818 by the *Illinois Emigrant* at Shawneetown. Schools, however, were few, primarily comprising informal private sessions

✧

The first Fort Dearborn was erected in 1803 and only stood until 1812 when it was destroyed during the war with England.
COURTESY OF THE CHICAGO HISTORICAL SOCIETY.
ENGRAVING; ICHI-21562

1 JOHN DEAN.   2 J. BAPTISTE BEAUBIEN.   3 FORT DEARBORN.   4 Dʳ WOLCOTT.   5 JOHN KINZIE.

CHICAGO IN 1831.

led by migrant teachers. Protestant ministers increased in number, including Baptists and Presbyterians, and by 1818 Methodists organized five circuits. The Catholic bishop of Bardstown, Kentucky, appointed a priest for Cahokia, where a Trappist monastery had been abandoned several years earlier.

By then, immigrants had begun locating on the less-desirable open and rolling prairies. For many months of the year those lands were wet and soft; the iron and wooden plows used by farmers in the east would not turn the black, sticky soil. In addition, mosquitoes in stagnant lakes and ponds produced frequent, sometimes deadly, outbreaks of malaria and typhoid fever. But as threats of disease gradually lessened, settlement continued increasing.

The U.S. Congress granted War of 1812 veterans certain lands in the new territories. The Illinois Military Tract comprised a 3.5-million-acre triangle of prairie, timber, and floodplain between the Mississippi and Illinois rivers. Although most soldiers or their heirs accepted the 160-acre tracts, few actually settled on the land, which was considered too far west and still in hostile territory. Many sold the bounties for $100 each to eastern speculators, who anticipated eventual land-value increases. One such investor acquired nine hundred thousand acres.

With the growing population, settlers in both Illinois Territory and Missouri began

agitating for statehood. In the Kaskaskia newspaper (renamed the *Western Intelligencer*), Daniel Pope Cook, the auditor of public accounts and an Edwards protégé, argued that Illinois, to the east, should precede Missouri achieving that status. In his 1817 annual message, Governor Edwards recommended statehood and within ten days, the legislators unanimously passed a petition to Congress.

As originally introduced, the petition identified the northern boundary at ten miles north of the southern end of Lake Michigan. Territorial delegate Nathaniel Pope appealed for a more generous portion of the shore, convinced that a Great Lakes port would bring eastern immigrants to the new state. As a result, the boundary was shifted some fifty miles northward, adding about eight thousand square miles to the territory of the state, including the site of Chicago and most of today's fourteen most populous and prosperous counties. Another Pope amendment provided that a portion of federal land revenues be allocated for education, assuring an advantage to Illinois citizens not then available in most other states.

Congress approved statehood in April 1818, and President James Monroe signed legislation enabling "the people of Illinois Territory to form a constitution and state government, and for the admission of such state into the union."

✧

An illustration depicting Fort Dearborn and the rapidly growing town of Chicago in 1831.

CHAPTER IV

THE FRONTIER STATE, 1818-1848

The hardy settlers came and dotted the little groves with their cabins and inclosures; their domestic animals increased rapidly on these rich pastures; and in a few years from the time the first dwelling was built on the border of a prairie, considerable herds of cattle and large droves of horses might be seen frolicking and feeding on it....

They had left the dense forests of Ohio and Pennsylvania, the undulating hills of Kentucky, and the old homes of Virginia, for the new and more hopeful country which adventurers assured them lay beyond.

- Eliza W. Farnham, *Life in Prairie Land* (1835-1839)

A century and a half after Louis Jolliet predicted future development of the prairies, residents of the Illinois Territory prepared for statehood. Population at the time was just under thirty-five thousand, primarily in the rich Mississippi River bottomlands and near the salines of southeastern Gallatin County.

A few white traders, along with about twelve thousand Kickapoo, Sauk and Fox, Winnebago, and Potawatomi, inhabited the northern and central areas. In northeastern Illinois, however, where natives had relinquished their lands, Chicago became an isolated outpost. "Aside from visits of traders with Mackinac goods," wrote historian Bessie Louise Pierce, "and the occasional passage of war parties to assail the American frontier, Chicago lapsed into a prairie wilderness."

The territorial center of Kaskaskia became the state's first capital. In a rented two-story brick residence, thirty-three delegates to the constitutional convention began discussing pertinent issues, among the most contentious being slavery and indenture. During the years of territorial government, many Illinoisans had petitioned Congress for repeal of indenture laws. An eventual compromise prohibited further introduction of slavery or involuntary servitude, but maintained the status of several hundred French slaves and life-indentured servants working in the southeastern salines, by then the largest industry in the west.

The new constitution, enacted in August, was brief and rudimentary, its writers having borrowed provisions from the federal and other state constitutions of the revolutionary period. The Illinois document provided for universal white male suffrage after six months' residence and gave the General Assembly power to direct state government, appointing all state officers other than the governor, lieutenant governor, and legislators.

In September, voters chose Shadrach Bond, the Illinois Territory's congressional delegate, as the state's first governor. The General Assembly elected Ninian Edwards and former Indiana legislator Jesse B. Thomas as United States senators, and John McLean of Shawneetown became the first congressman.

After the U.S. Congress approved the state's constitution, President Monroe on December 3, 1818, signed the act admitting Illinois as the twenty-first state in the Union. "We will enter upon a state government," wrote convention delegate Nathaniel Pope, "with better prospects than any state ever did—the best soil in the world, a mild climate, a large state with the most ample funds to educate every child in the state."

In accordance with the 1785 federal land ordinance, surveyors plotted the state into rectangular townships and sections, beginning on the Mississippi near Alton, east to the Third Principal Meridian, south thirty miles to the base line, east again to the southwest corner of the Vincennes tract, then northeastward to the Indiana line near present Vermilion and Edgar counties.

✧

Before railroads were built in Illinois, river transit was the main form of transportation to and within Illinois. Most settlers arrived in boats and soon developed a large system of waterway transport. Water crafts were used for commerce, trade, and even housing.

COURTESY OF THE CHICAGO HISTORICAL SOCIETY. CREATOR - CURRIER & IVES. PHOTOGRAPHIC PRINT, ICHI-07667.

The most densely settled region remained the American Bottom. Many of those inhabitants came from the upland south, descendants of seventeenth- and early eighteenth-century Scottish, English, and Scotch-Irish immigrants. Within a few years of statehood, Kaskaskia counted nearly one thousand inhabitants. Its weekly newspaper contained advertisements for nine general stores, three tailor shops, and a tavern.

✧
The first schoolhouse in Springfield, Illinois
COURTESY OF THE SANGAMON VALLEY COLLECTION AT LINCOLN LIBRARY, SPRINGFIELD.

Several hundred British farmers, led by Quaker Morris Birkbeck and his friend George Flower, settled in a grassland region of Edwards County, north of Shawneetown. Birkbeck wrote several books and pamphlets for British emigrants, and from 1818 to 1820 many travelers to the United States visited his colony. Rejecting claims by southern frontiersmen that the Illinois prairie could not be profitably farmed, he maintained that the soil, once broken, was the richest in America. By 1819 the settlement included four hundred English and seven hundred Americans, and that year Birkbeck became president of the state's first organization to promote scientific agriculture.

In addition to river transportation, land travel was important in the state's development. By 1818 trails connected Shawneetown and the village of Golconda with Kaskaskia. Settlers north of the capital established the Goshen Road, a 150-mile path from Shawneetown to Edwardsville. Other trails led from the Ohio River to Cahokia, Vincennes to St. Louis, Shawneetown to the English settlement, Kaskaskia (by way of Belleville) to Edwardsville, and Kaskaskia to Peoria. All were made, as George Flower wrote, "by one man on horseback following in the track of another, every rider making the way a little easier to find,

until you came to some slush, or swampy place, where all trace was lost, and you got through as others had done, by guessing at the direction, often riding at hazard for miles until you stumbled on the track again."

When the Illinois General Assembly met in 1819, members enacted a series of measures restricting the liberty of blacks and mulattoes, which became known as the Black Code. Enforcement of these laws would continue for more than four decades. Slaves could not be brought into Illinois for emancipation, and indentured servants, treated as mere property, were not allowed to vote, serve on juries, or testify in court against white persons.

In 1820, pro-slavery Illinois Senator Jesse B. Thomas led efforts for passage of the Missouri Compromise, combining the admission of Maine as a free state with Missouri as a slave state in order to maintain a balance between the free and slave states. After Missouri attained statehood, southern Illinois settlers were nearly surrounded by areas of slavery.

In 1824 a group of citizens agitated for legalized slavery for the Shawneetown salines, but newly elected Governor Edward Coles, aided by members of Birkbeck's English community, opposed the effort. Coles, an emigrant from Virginia, had freed his own seventeen slaves, giving each family a quarter section of farmland he owned near Edwardsville. Through his efforts, voters defeated the call for a pro-slavery constitutional convention, yet the buying and selling of slaves continued. Between 1829 and 1833 the General Assembly enacted measures regarding runaway slaves, prohibiting marriage between blacks and whites, and prohibiting black children from attending school with whites.

About ten years after Coles freed his own slaves, two settlements of free blacks were among the earliest such communities in the United States. In 1829 a former Kentucky slave, Francis "Free Frank" McWorter, settled in Pike County and established the biracial town of New Philadelphia. At about the same time, the village of Brooklyn in the American Bottom of St. Clair County attracted both free and fugitive blacks. New Philadelphia thrived for more than fifty years, but the lack of a

railroad line contributed to its eventual demise. Brooklyn would evolve into a community for blacks working in nearby industrial towns.

In the Chicago area, fur trader Gurdon S. Hubbard purchased the American Fur Company's property and became one of the town's first entrepreneurs. The Hubbard's Trail he blazed between Chicago and his residence in Danville eventually became a state road, which in Chicago was named State Street. The 1825 opening of the Erie Canal in New York provided a new route for transporting travelers and goods from the eastern states through the Great Lakes to Chicago. Within a few years, the once small settlement would surpass Shawneetown as the state's principal port of entry.

Northwestern Illinois also benefited from increasing commerce and the Erie Canal. Galena, with only four log houses in 1826, grew rapidly into the largest city north of St. Louis, a supply center for lead mines in Illinois, Iowa, and Wisconsin and a busy shipping point for Mississippi River trade.

From a frontier society, Illinois was developing into an expanding community of villages, cities, churches, and newspapers. Brick and frame houses replaced the log cabins of territorial days. Local merchants offered hardware, rifles, powder, blankets,

and yard goods, along with wines, cigars, spices, fruits, jewelry, linens, and silks.

As settled areas of the state expanded, the General Assembly voted to relocate the capital. The members chose Vandalia, eighty-five miles northeast of Kaskaskia, along the Kaskaskia River. State government at that time consisted merely of a biennial legislature, several administrative officials, and a court system.

In 1821, legislators chartered a state bank at Vandalia, with branches in Shawneetown, Edwardsville, and Brownsville. Then at Shawneetown in 1836, a red-brick Greek Revival bank building replaced the small log structure. Philadelphia-born lawyer and War of 1812 veteran James Hall became state treasurer. In addition to a prospering legal practice, Hall served as editor of the state's second newspaper, the *Illinois Gazette*, and in 1830 founded a periodical, *Illinois Monthly Magazine*. The first newspaper published outside the southern counties was the *Galena Miners' Journal* in 1828, followed by the *Chicago Democrat* in 1833. Two years later the daily *Chicago American* was founded, and by 1839 thirty-six newspapers were reported in the state—mostly associated with a political faction or party.

Political leadership during the early years of statehood was aristocratic and based on family, primarily southern, alliances. The informal judiciary generally involved simple cases brought by often self-taught lawyers. "Out of the long list of Lawyers that come to this country and settle," wrote Jacksonville attorney Stephen A. Douglas in 1835, "there is not one out of an hundred who does one half the business enough to pay his expenses the first year."

In the mid-1830s, the national Democratic and Whig parties gained stature in Illinois. The Democrats had already adopted the convention system of nomination for public office, and Douglas' strong party leadership led to control of the state legislature and election of two decades of Democratic governors. An emerging Whig leader, Kentucky native Abraham Lincoln, was a surveyor, postmaster at the small central Illinois village of New Salem, and a lawyer. Elected in 1834 to the first of four

✧

Possibly the first photograph of Abraham Lincoln, at a time when he was active in Illinois electoral politics.

COURTESY OF THE CHICAGO HISTORICAL SOCIETY. PHOTOGRAPH, ICHI-30366.

terms in the state legislature, Lincoln became an avid follower of Kentucky's U.S. Senator, Henry Clay, advocating the Whig "American system" of internal improvements, protective tariffs, and economic modernization.

Increasing immigration into northern and western Illinois gradually forced remaining Sauk and Fox across the Mississippi River. In 1832, the courageous Sauk warrior Black Hawk and fifteen hundred of his followers returned to the state to plant seasonal crops. Defining the action as an invasion, Governor John Reynolds called for their expulsion by state and federal troops. As terrorized settlers fled, the military fought several battles and skirmishes in northern Illinois and southern Wisconsin. After fifteen weeks, the badly outnumbered Sauk and Fox were trapped on the shore of Bad Axe River in Wisconsin. Several hundred were killed, Black Hawk and two sons were captured, and most of the few survivors surrendered. Their defeat, along with Potawatomi land cessions the following year, marked the passing of Native Americans from Illinois.

During the first thirty years of statehood, frontier life focused on material rather than intellectual pursuits. Thus, few residents were interested in formal education for their families. One settler noted that most parents found arithmetic unnecessary and grammar of no use to anyone "who could talk so as to be understood by everybody."

Still, some settlers began efforts to bring learning and culture to the frontier. The basic subjects of reading, writing, and arithmetic were offered at subscription-based private schools. Female education generally consisted of needlework, painting, or other domestic subjects. A minister taught Latin and French in Kaskaskia, while an endowment provided free public education in Alton. In 1829 the General Assembly repealed the state law allowing localities to levy taxes for public education, and another would not be passed until 1845.

In Vandalia, a secondary-level private school opened in 1830 with a female department and woman instructor. That year Methodist preacher Peter Cartwright advertised a school in the central Illinois village of Pleasant Plains, offering elementary subjects, Latin, Greek, and moral philosophy. Cartwright, a charismatic orator who converted hundreds at camp meetings, twice won election to the state legislature.

Higher education began in 1827, when John Mason Peck, the first Baptist missionary in the west, opened a theological training school at Rock Spring, near Shiloh in St. Clair County. Within four years the school was moved to Alton and in 1836 became Shurtleff College, named for a benefactor. Cartwright helped found the Methodist McKendree College in Lebanon, which accepted female students. In 1829 four Yale Theological

❖

A log cabin built by Abraham Lincoln's
parents on Goose Nest Prairie
near Charleston, Illinois, in 1831.

Seminary students established Illinois College in Jacksonville, a town of twelve hundred and seat of the state's most populous county.

Jonathan Baldwin Turner, a brother of one of the Yale band, came to Illinois College in 1835 as an instructor in Latin and Greek. Turner established the *Illinois Statesman*, an intellectual, antislavery, and political periodical. An advocate for wildlife and natural resource conservation, he invented agricultural implements and developed techniques to help farmers and fruit growers.

Also in 1835, the General Assembly granted a charter for the first women's educational institution, the Jacksonville Female Academy. Episcopal Bishop Philander Chase opened Jubilee College in Peoria County, with a seminary, classical preparatory school for boys and girls, and small farming operations. In Galesburg, New York Presbyterian minister George Washington Gale organized the Knox Manual Labor College, which opened in 1837. By the early 1840s, the state had twelve colleges, but only Illinois College granted degrees.

Roman Catholic settlers gradually reestablished their religion, which had nearly disappeared after the American Revolution. In 1808, the Illinois Territory was included in the diocese of Bardstown, Kentucky. Successive dioceses that included Illinois were founded at Vincennes and St. Louis. In 1833 a priest was assigned to the approximately one hundred French-Canadian and Indian Catholics in the Chicago area, and in 1844 Chicago became the diocese for all of Illinois.

A few African-American churches, principally Methodist and Baptist, were also organized. The Wood River Colored Baptist Association, the first such organization in Illinois, began in 1839 with members from St. Clair and Madison counties, later expanding to include churches as far distant as Salem and Decatur.

The first Amish settlers arrived in 1831 from the French provinces of Alsace and Lorraine, seeking religious freedom in the timbered lands of the Illinois River in Woodford, Tazewell, and Bureau counties. In the mid-1860s the Amish moved to prairie farms in east central Illinois, where members

today still follow ancestral practices and shun most conveniences of modern society.

In 1829 the state-authorized Canal Commission began planning a waterway that would connect Lake Michigan and the Chicago River with the Illinois River, then via the Mississippi to the Gulf of Mexico. Ottawa, at the junction of the Illinois and Fox rivers, was the first town to be plotted, followed in 1830 by Chicago, at the other end of the proposed canal.

By the early 1830s, steamboats brought streams of eastern immigrants as well as German farmers and Irish laborers to the fertile prairies of central and northern Illinois, gradually challenging the state's southern dominance. New Englanders concentrated in the northern sections, where they found the prairie soil amenable for commercial agriculture and the waterfalls of the Rock and Fox rivers suitable for manufacturing operations.

The state's population nearly tripled during the 1830s. As land sellers and buyers thronged into the area by steamboat and stagecoach, more than five hundred new towns were laid out between 1835 and 1837. Established cities of Quincy, Peoria, Rushville, Peru, Ottawa, Joliet, Elgin, St. Charles, and Rockford grew in size and variety of services.

In 1834 the number of Chicago residents reached eighteen hundred, but by 1837, when

❖

Illinois State University at Springfield was one of the many schools built in Illinois during the academic surge of the mid-1800s.

the city received a charter, Europeans and easterners arriving by way of the Erie Canal increased the population to more than four thousand. A former New York state senator, William B. Ogden, won the first mayoral election, 469 to 237, over the only other candidate, John Harris Kinzie, son of the early trader.

In both 1836 and 1837 the General Assembly approved massive "internal improvement" measures, including funding for the Illinois and Michigan Canal, along with eight state-owned railway lines. The cost was estimated at nearly $10 million. Land and real estate speculators flocked to Chicago, anticipating its commercial dominance of the Midwest.

In July 1836, construction began on the canal, funded by state-approved loans. The following year, work was started on the first railroad, the Northern Cross, an eastward route from Quincy to the Indiana border. Within only a few weeks, however, the financial panic of 1837 and ensuing severe depression resulted in bank failures and the cessation of work on both the railroad and canal. The General Assembly struggled with the crisis for several years, until legislators approved property-tax levies and debt-repayment plans.

As a reflection of the changing demography, in 1837 the General Assembly considered moving the capital from Vandalia to a more central location. Stephen Douglas favored Jacksonville, but Abraham Lincoln and other Whigs won a majority vote for Springfield, a town of about eleven hundred. The new capital was incorporated as a city in 1840, with a $260,000 statehouse constructed on the public square.

In Grand Detour, in northern Illinois, Vermont emigré John Deere in 1837 invented a self-cleaning steel plow that cut through the dense prairie sod, allowing farmers to cultivate more land for larger crop yields. Inventor Cyrus Hall McCormick, a Virginia native, designed a reaper with which two workers could perform the amount of cultivation that previously required the effort of ten men. Opening a factory in Chicago in 1847, he sold the machines with product guarantees and deferred payment plans.

About the same time, Deere moved his plow-making plant to Moline, and within ten years was producing ten thousand plows annually for farmers throughout the nation.

In 1830, President Andrew Jackson had signed the Indian Removal Act to relocate eastern tribes to territory west of the Mississippi and take possession of the eastern lands for settlement. For nearly three months in 1838-1839, some eight thousand Cherokee, forced from their tribal homes in Georgia, North Carolina, Alabama, and Tennessee, trekked through southern Illinois from Golconda to Jonesboro, a portion of the grueling "Trail of Tears" to reservations in Oklahoma. Many perished on the trip from the frigid weather, hunger, and disease.

As a further stimulus to westward migration, in 1839 the National Road, authorized early in the century by President Thomas Jefferson, stretched nearly six hundred miles from Cumberland, Maryland, to Vandalia. Along the ninety-mile route in Illinois, travelers found shops and lodging in new towns that included Effingham, Teutopolis, and Marshall. Within a few decades, however, the once-bustling highway fell into disrepair, surpassed by more dependable and economical river and railroad transportation systems.

By 1840, all of the state, except for a small east-central section, reported at least two inhabitants per square mile. Population was most dense on the western side, extending from Quincy to Jacksonville, then south into Madison and St. Clair counties. In 1842 a young Charles Dickens visited southern Illinois and published his observations in a travel book titled *American Notes*. He described Cairo as a "detestable morass" and Belleville as "a small collection of wooden houses, huddled together in the very heart of the bush and swamp." A Belleville hotel appeared to Dickens as "an odd shambling, low-roofed out-house, half cowshed and half kitchen"—a not uncommon appraisal from European travelers.

The southern tip of Illinois became known as Egypt, with town names including Cairo, Karnak, and Thebes. Some attribute the nickname to the northern Illinois droughts in the 1840s, when area farmers provided corn and wheat—just as in ancient times, Egypt had supplied grain to neighboring countries. The mild climate of Illinois' Egypt was suited to fruit cultivation, and, for a time in mid-century, tobacco was also an important crop.

In northeastern Illinois, construction of the Illinois and Michigan Canal resumed in the early 1840s, with an influx of Irish immigrant laborers. Completed in 1848, the 96-mile canal and series of locks carried vessels transporting agricultural goods from the Illinois River Valley to Chicago, then by the Great Lakes to eastern and Canadian ports. In exchange, manufactured goods flowed down the canal from Chicago into the Mississippi River system. The city stretched for three and a half miles along Lake Michigan, with approximately 17,000 inhabitants. During the canal's first seven years of operation, Chicago's population grew to 80,000 and by 1860 would be nearly 110,000. Newly established towns along the canal route also increased commerce between east and west.

In 1839, facing hostility from neighbors in Missouri, thousands of members of the Church of Jesus Christ of Latter-day Saints, or Mormons, moved across the Mississippi to Adams and Hancock counties. Led by the

✧

Cyrus Hall McCormick's mechanical reaper, patented in 1834, revolutionized the farming industry by allowing fewer farmers to harvest more than they could by hand.

COURTESY OF THE CHICAGO HISTORICAL SOCIETY. CREATOR - CURRIER & IVES, AFTER DRAWING BY FRANCES. LITHOGRAPH; ICHI-29626

religious prophet Joseph Smith, they selected a town along the river, Nauvoo, as the church's new center. The Illinois General Assembly, with support from both political parties, granted the Mormons a charter that made the city virtually independent of state government, even authorizing a private militia, the Nauvoo Legion. In 1841, church members began constructing the Nauvoo Temple, and by 1844, Nauvoo, with some twelve thousand inhabitants, developed into the state's largest city.

That year Smith alienated both Democratic and Whig politicians by declaring his candidacy for the U.S. presidency. He also became the focus of resentment among dissidents and anti-Mormons. After his Nauvoo Legion was accused of destroying the opposition *Nauvoo Expositor* newspaper, Governor Thomas Ford sent the state militia to restore order and arrest Smith and his brother Hyrum. But Ford failed to protect the prisoners. While they were confined in the county jail at Carthage, a mob broke in and murdered both men.

The Mormons dedicated their temple in 1846, but following a bitter organizational struggle and continuing anti-Mormon fervor in the area, they left Illinois that year. Most followed their new prophet, Brigham Young,

in search of a home in the far west. Two years later, a dissident set fire to their temple.

For about fifteen years beginning in the 1840s, a charismatic Swedish pietist, Eric Janson, and four hundred followers maintained a utopian communal religious settlement in Henry County. Although the settlement's tight organization deteriorated after Janson's death in 1850, Bishop Hill grew into a thriving community of more than a thousand members, constructing large brick buildings and harvesting flax, wheat, and sorghum. Area residents purchased colony members' linens, wool fabrics, rugs, furniture, implements, meat, dairy, and agricultural products.

While many residents of southern Illinois continued to support slavery and indenture, abolitionism in the state was championed by Elijah P. Lovejoy, a zealous Presbyterian preacher and editor of the antislavery *Alton Observer*. He established the Illinois Anti-Slavery Society in 1837, with ninety-nine delegates from sixteen counties attending the first annual meeting. Members formulated plans to establish county and town organizations, along with antislavery newspapers and almanacs, in order to petition for repeal of the Black Code. Later that year, however, an enraged pro-slavery mob shot and killed Lovejoy and destroyed his printing office.

Anti-Slavery Society members attained better success in central and northern Illinois. In Princeton, Lovejoy's brother Owen helped escaping blacks, and in Quincy, Presbyterian minister David Nelson operated an abolitionist institute for missionary training.

In 1841, state legislators ended the selling of indentured servants, yet free blacks still could not vote, sue, testify in courts, or serve in the militia. Some were even kidnapped and shipped south into slavery. Anti-Slavery Society members petitioned the United States Senate for abolition throughout the country, preparing Illinois supporters for a prominent role in the momentous antislavery conflict to follow.

Quincy physician Richard Eells was convicted in 1842 for sheltering fugitive slaves, after which the *Quincy Whig* commented, "We hope this will prove a warning to the abolitionists for the future." Still, a growing number of Illinoisans disregarded the laws against harboring and assisting fugitive slaves—although their "underground railroad"

was poorly operated and most runaways were eventually apprehended.

After the United States annexed the territory of Texas in 1845, Mexican troops crossed into a disputed area north of the Rio Grande River and shelled an American fort. President James K. Polk pronounced the action an invasion of U.S. soil, and Congress declared a state of war. Newly elected Illinois Whig Representative Abraham Lincoln, who vigorously opposed the action, supported the 1846 Wilmot Proviso— an amendment stipulating that no war-acquired territory be open to slavery. House members passed the bill, but it was defeated in the Senate. Governor Ford sent six regiments to Texas, where one hundred Illinois soldiers lost their lives.

By mid-century, Illinois had passed from a frontier land to one of bustling cities and towns, prosperous prairie farms, schools and institutions of higher learning, and a transportation system of steamboats, stagecoaches, railroads, and the newly completed Illinois and Michigan Canal. The success of that and other midwest canals would last but a few years, however, with the onset of railroads.

In Chicago, two editors and a merchant in 1847 established the *Daily Tribune*, the city's third newspaper. Businessman John S. Wright, founder of *Prairie Farmer* magazine, financed the city's first public school building and strongly advocated improved educational opportunities throughout the state. "We believe that at least three-fourths of the teachers in the common schools of Illinois could not pass an examination in the rudiments of the English language," he wrote, "and most of them have taken to teaching because they hadn't anything in particular to do." In 1845 Wright supported legislation that created the office of state superintendent of public instruction and designated congressional townships as school townships, allowing voters within the districts to approve education taxation.

A new constitution adopted in 1848 was three times the length of the original. It changed the structure of Illinois government by limiting the power of the legislature and increasing that of the governor, as well as providing for township government within counties.

✧

Owen Lovejoy dedicated his life to the abolition of slavery after his brother Elijah was killed by a mob of pro-slavery advocates. Owen's home became an important station on Illinois' Underground Railroad. He worked in the ministry at Hampshire Colony Congregational Church for seventeen years, preaching his views against slavery. He eventually felt the need to enter politics to fulfill his life's purpose and was elected to the Illinois legislature in 1854 and later served as a senator for four successive terms.

CHAPTER V

DOUGLAS, LINCOLN & THE CIVIL WAR ERA, 1848-1870

The settlers were hard at work with axe and plough; yet, in spite of material pre-occupation, all felt the unnameable influence of unfolding destiny. The social cycle, which began with the Declaration of Independence, was drawing to a close....

Swiftly and silently came the mighty influences. Thousands laboured on in silence; thousands were acting under an imperative, spiritual impulse without knowing it; the whole country round about Springfield was being illuminated by the genius of one man, Abraham Lincoln, whose influence penetrated all hearts, creeds, parties, and institutions.

- Francis Grierson, *The Valley of Shadows*

The late 1840s began a new era in Illinois settlement and commerce. When writer Francis Grierson arrived in the 1850s, the prairie population had doubled, with immigrants not only from northern Europe but also from eastern and southern states. Within ten years, Illinois ranked first in the nation in both corn and wheat production. Northern areas provided most of the state's oat and rye crops, while apples, peaches, and melons were cultivated in central and southern Illinois.

Farmers in many counties organized agricultural associations and in 1853 established the Illinois State Agricultural Society. Members held their first state fair that year in Springfield, which in 1893 became the permanent state fair location, after annual exhibitions at locations throughout the state.

The river towns of the forties swelled into thriving cities, and a network of railroads would soon revolutionize life on the Illinois prairie, providing a more efficient transportation system than the riverways or the dirt and plank roads. In 1850 organizers of the Illinois Central Railroad received the federal government's first construction land grant and within six years built the world's largest rail line, a 750-mile route connecting Chicago with Galena and Cairo. In 1856 the first railroad bridge across the Mississippi opened at Rock Island, a milestone in American westward migration.

On the Illinois River in central Illinois, Peoria evolved into a commercial center and during the 1850s would surpass Galena as the state's second largest city. Populations swelled throughout Illinois, but the growth of Chicago was phenomenal. Already the busiest port in America, by 1856 the city became the nation's transportation hub, with shipping docks for the Illinois and Michigan Canal and a four-thousand-mile network of railroad track. The population of eighty-four thousand—double the number of only four years earlier—included throngs of European immigrants and easterners drawn to the city's commerce and jobs. By 1860, Chicago's 112,000 population included more foreign-born than native-born residents.

During the 1850s, larger cities began providing public utilities, including gas-lit streets. Until pure water supplies, adequate drainage, and sewers became available in the 1860s and 1870s, however, disease resulting from stagnant water and lack of sanitation remained a chronic problem.

After the state legislature in 1855 provided for free local public schools, educational progress was rapid. Jacksonville opened the first public high school, and Springfield established a public school system that included a separate facility for black children. In 1855 a group of Methodist businessmen opened Northwestern University in Evanston as an institution free of corrupting urban and saloon influences. Two years later the General Assembly granted a charter to Northwestern and established Illinois State Normal School, near Bloomington, as the state's first teacher-training institution.

Lectures on cultural and religious subjects became popular, often sponsored by literary clubs. A widespread movement for local libraries began early in the 1850s; and within twenty years the state would report fourteen thousand libraries, including a state library (established at Springfield in

❖

Due to the large number of immigrant workers and ready access to rail lines, Chicago was a prime location for the Union Stockyards, which opened in 1865.

COURTESY OF THE CHICAGO HISTORICAL SOCIETY. LITHOGRAPHER - JEVNE & ALMINI. LITHOGRAPH, 1866, ICHI-06898

1839), seven historical, literary, or scientific facilities, and more than three thousand school and college libraries. In 1856, Chicagoans organized the Chicago Historical Society, which soon housed a collection of eleven thousand volumes, primarily gifts from Society members and friends.

Chicago's first symphony orchestra and the Chicago Musical Union were formed in the mid-1850s. Belleville supported a philharmonic orchestra, while concert and dance halls were popular in towns both large and small. Sporting events also drew crowds, including a Chicago baseball club organized in 1856.

Immigrants continued flooding into the state, including many who fled an unsuccessful revolution in Germany and settled primarily in Chicago, Belleville, Galena, Quincy, Alton, Peoria, and Peru. Large numbers of Scandinavians came principally to Chicago, Rockford, Moline, and Galesburg. Among towns with French and French-Canadians settlers were Kankakee, Beardstown, and Ottawa.

Etienne Cabet, founder of a French communal group known as Icarians, acquired the deserted Mormon property at Nauvoo. His five hundred members established a school and newspaper, and operated mills, stores, and distilleries. The community thrived for only a few years, however, before factional quarrels caused its dissolution. Between 1858 and 1860 some members, including Cabet, moved to Missouri, while others went to Iowa. Following the Icarian departure, German and Swiss immigrants planted vineyards at Nauvoo and within twenty years were major wine producers.

The steady growth of Yankee-dominated northern Illinois brought polarizing changes in the state, although men and women of all viewpoints lived throughout the state. Southern sympathizers were more abundant in southern Illinois, while a larger number of free-soilers and abolitionists resided in the northern sections. Most citizens either held opinions between the extremes or expressed no judgment on the slavery issue. The 1850 federal census for the first time listed no blacks as slaves in Illinois, yet the General Assembly in 1853 again prohibited free blacks from settling

in the state. One historian described that legislation as "undoubtedly the most severe anti-Negro measure passed by a free state."

The following year Democratic Illinois Senator Stephen A. Douglas was a leading supporter of the Kansas-Nebraska Act, espousing the "popular sovereignty" principle that residents of each territory should decide the slavery issue. The act overturned the Missouri Compromise and established slavery in Kansas Territory. Resulting disunity among Democrats and disintegration of the Whig party led to a national coalition of Whigs, antislavery Democrats, and Know-Nothings, a secret organization whose members opposed the Irish and other Catholic immigrants. Efforts of the alliance culminated in a new Republican party, based on opposition to the expansion of slavery. During the party's national convention in 1856, former Illinois congressman Abraham Lincoln received 110 votes on a preliminary ballot for the vice-presidential nomination.

In Illinois that year, the Democrats held a small majority in the legislature, but Democrat-turned-Republican William H. Bissell was elected the first in a long series of Republican governors. During the senatorial race of 1858, incumbent Douglas reiterated his strong support for the Kansas-Nebraska Act. Lincoln, his Republican opponent, warned that slavery might be inevitable in

Illinois. "A house divided against itself cannot stand," Lincoln declared in accepting the party's nomination. "I believe this government cannot endure, permanently half slave and half free." Either those who opposed slavery would cause its extinction, he argued, "or its advocates will push it forward, till it shall become alike lawful in all the States, old as well as new-North as well as South."

The candidates held joint debates in seven of the state's congressional districts—primarily centered on the slavery issue.

At Freeport, Southern Democrats were enraged by Douglas' assertion that residents of a territory could exclude slavery. On the grounds of Knox College in Galesburg, Lincoln said of Douglas, "He is blowing out the moral lights around us, when he contends that whoever wants slaves has a right to hold them." Douglas won the election, but eastern newspaper coverage of the debates established Lincoln as a national figure.

In May 1860, the Republican National Convention met in a Chicago hall known as the Wigwam, at the corner of Wacker Drive and Lake Street. With major support from the *Chicago Tribune*'s Joseph Medill, Lincoln edged out New York Senator William Seward and other eastern hopefuls to win the party's presidential nomination. Douglas, his senatorial rival, was nominated by the northern wing of the national Democratic party. Declaring "important principles may, and must be inflexible," Lincoln defeated Senator Douglas and two other candidates to become the sixteenth president of the United States. In Illinois, Lincoln won 70 percent of the vote in northern counties, but only 20 percent in the far southern sections.

Even before he took office, southern states began seceding from the Union. Then within weeks of his March 4, 1861, inauguration, the enmity between north and south over states' rights and slavery erupted into Civil War. Confederate forces fired on Fort Sumter, in the harbor of Charleston, South Carolina, forcing surrender of the federal troops. President Lincoln's secretary of war called on Illinois' antislavery Republican governor, Richard Yates, for the immediate service of six militia regiments, and Douglas appealed to his followers to uphold the government. "This rebellion is a prodigious crime," he told state legislators, "and the shortest way to peace is the most unanimous and stupendous preparation for war."

By fall of 1861 thousands of Illinoisans volunteered, including many farm workers, all of whom expected the war to be brief and illustrious. Despite resulting labor shortages, farmers' McCormick harvesters increased needed wheat production. "Without McCormick's invention," remarked Secretary of War Edwin Stanton, "I feel the North could not win, that the Union would be dismembered." More than six thousand Illinois Germans joined the Union army, as regiments were organized by nationality, ethnicity, occupation, and even religion. By October, Illinois provided more regiments than even New York.

✧

Political cartoon "Honest old Abe on the Stump, Springfield 1858." Lincoln is portrayed by his Democratic opponents as being "two-faced" in his decision to seek the presidency.

COURTESY OF THE CHICAGO HISTORICAL SOCIETY. CREATOR - R.R. WILSON.

Honest old Abe on the Stump. Springfield 1858.

Honest old Abe on the Stump, at the ratification Meeting of Presidential Nominations. Springfield 1860.

But Illinois was caught in the intense North-South schism. Although most citizens continued holding moderate opinions in support of the Union, reports were rampant during the early months of "disunionist" sentiment in the Marion and Carbondale areas of far southern Illinois. Two downstate newspapers, the *Jonesboro Gazette* and the *Cairo City Gazette*, were openly secessionist. Some area residents joined the secret, anti-war Knights of the Golden Circle, helping the organization become a formidable political faction. Countering the pro-southern sentiments were zealous, sometimes violent abolitionists who insisted on a federal emancipation edict. President Lincoln refused their demand, not wanting to alienate loyal border states.

Most Illinois troops received training at Camp Douglas on the southern edge of Chicago or at Camp Butler, east of Springfield. Both soon also became Confederate prison camps. Other Confederate prisoners would be guarded in an old penitentiary at Alton or at Rock Island, site of a federal arsenal built in 1862.

Lincoln's first general officers included former Democratic Congressman John A. McClernand, an influential figure in southern Illinois. Despite Lincoln's admonition that McClernand "keep Egypt right side up," about forty-five men crossed into Kentucky and enlisted in the Confederate army. Through the course of the war, McClernand would

command an expedition in the 1863 Vicksburg, Mississippi, campaign and later participate in the successful Union advance on the city, effectively controlling all Mississippi River traffic and dividing the Confederacy.

Governor Yates also helped contain southern sympathies. Warned by the War Department of Cairo's strategic importance at the junction of the Ohio and Mississippi rivers, Yates sent nearly six hundred men from local militia units. He made several trips to New York and Washington in search of protection for Cairo, persuading federal government

officials to provide several thousand muskets, along with rifles and cannon.

As the war entered its second year, major Confederate victories and mounting casualties caused flagging morale among Unionists. In the summer of 1862, Republicans founded the Union League of America at Pekin, to combat anti-war propaganda of the Knights of the Golden Circle and to counter northern disillusionment with Lincoln's military policies. The Union League developed into a statewide and then a national organization, attracting 140,000 members in Illinois and nearly one million nationwide.

Hoping to not only deplete Southern slave reserves but also enhance the Union cause abroad, in January 1863, President Lincoln issued an executive order known as the Emancipation Proclamation. The document abolished slavery in the eleven Confederate states "as a fit and necessary war measure for suppressing said rebellion." Then as war fervor continued to wane and enlistments lagged, Lincoln approved the nation's first Conscription Act, ordering able-bodied men into military service.

In the autumn of 1863, Illinois' first black regiment was organized at Quincy. Eventually called the Twenty-ninth U.S. Colored Infantry, in the spring of 1864 the recruit regiment was assigned to the Fourth Division, IX Corps— the first black division to serve with the Union army in Virginia. After action at Petersburg, the Twenty-ninth participated in the final Confederate defeat at Appomattox. Illinois blacks served in twenty-one other

regiments, in artillery units, and in various regiments from several states.

Many women operated the family farms and sewed uniforms, and some served as traveling nurses. Mary "Mother" Bickerdyke, a Galesburg widow and nurse, helped in Cairo hospitals and in nineteen major battles. Chicago author Mary Livermore worked with the United States Sanitary Commission, helping improve conditions for sick and wounded troops. She later reported that a number of women passed as soldiers, among them Albert D. J. Cashier in the Ninety-fifth Illinois, who participated in several battles and years later was found to be a Livingston County Irish immigrant named Jennie Hodgers.

By the 1864 presidential campaign, Union and Confederate armies were locked in fierce, costly battles. Delegates to the Democratic National Convention in Chicago nominated Union general George B. McClellan as their presidential candidate. President Lincoln, who still held a deep core of northern support, won the election, as did Republican Richard J. Oglesby of Decatur as Illinois governor (the first of three Civil War generals to become governor of the state). His predecessor, Richard Yates, won election as U.S. senator. With these victories, Republicans made as their war aim the total abolition of slavery.

During the four-year Civil War, nearly 260,000 Illinois troops served in Union armies, a total exceeded only by New York, Pennsylvania, and Ohio. The men fought in many of the war's bloodiest battles: Chickamauga, Shiloh, Corinth, Murphreesboro, Vicksburg, and Chattanooga,

✧

Above: Group portrait of confederate prisoners held as POW's at Camp Douglas, considered one of the war's more humane prisoner camps.
COURTESY OF THE CHICAGO HISTORICAL SOCIETY. PHOTOGRAPH, 1863; ICHI-01800.

Below: A powerful brigadier general during the Civil War, Ulysses S. Grant, of Galena, Illinois, became a symbol of Union victory and was a logical candidate for the 1868 presidential election. He became the eighteenth president of the United States.
COURTESY OF THE CHICAGO HISTORICAL SOCIETY. PHOTOGRAPH, ICHI-10525.

and many lesser engagements. Seventy Illinois regiments participated in General William T. Sherman's devastating 1864 campaign through Georgia. Thirty-five thousand Illinois men and boys died in battle, of wounds or disease, or in prison camps.

General Ulysses S. Grant, a Mexican War soldier who began his Union service at Galena, ended the war as commander of all Union armies. Among the scores of Illinois officers who helped lead Union forces were generals McClernand, Oglesby, Benjamin H. Grierson of Jacksonville, Stephen A. Hurlbut of Belvidere, John A. Logan of Murphysboro, John M. Palmer of Springfield, and Benjamin Prentiss of Quincy.

Both Governor Oglesby and Senator Yates recommended repeal of the state's anti-black laws, as well as an abolition provision in the U.S. Constitution. In February 1865, Illinois became the first state in the nation to ratify the Thirteenth Amendment, which abolished slavery. At the same session, legislators repealed the state's repressive black laws that had existed in varying forms since statehood.

Then, in early April, Union forces occupied the Confederate capital of Richmond, Virginia. "Grant's and Lincoln's names were on everyone's lips," wrote historian Arthur Charles Cole. "Citizens proudly rejoiced that Illinois had contributed not only the largest

quotas of men but two loyal sons who as civil magistrate and as military leader had conducted the union cause to victory."

Soon after General Lee surrendered the Confederate army, the nation's rejoicing turned to despair. On April 14, 1865, President Lincoln, who planned conciliatory postwar reconstruction of the South, was assassinated by actor and Confederate sympathizer John Wilkes Booth, "just as he was to accomplish," grieved the *Cairo Morning News*, "the grandest and most solemn problem of statesmanship in the history of the world."

A special black-swathed funeral train slowly carried Lincoln's body to Illinois along the same route by which he had traveled to Washington four years earlier. In Springfield, the casket lay in state in the capitol before burial at Oak Ridge Cemetery.

The war years generated a dynamic agricultural, industrial, and economic expansion in Illinois. New factories produced munitions and supplies for the armies as well as a variety of consumer goods. In the eastern Illinois town of Charleston, planning for the Charleston & Danville Railroad gave the "people new zeal" in constructing "several fine buildings, business houses and dwellings." By 1870 the state's total miles of track ranked first among the states.

Corn, wheat, and swine production increased, and stockyards were built along rail lines. Coal and iron were shipped to the centrally located smelters of Chicago, where the nation's first steel rails were produced at the Chicago Rolling Mills. The Board of Trade, which opened in 1848 as a central

✧

Above: President Lincoln's funeral procession left Washington, D.C., on April 21, 1865, bound for Springfield, Illinois, his home during much of his political career. He lay in state at the state capitol, shown here with funeral bunting. Lincoln was buried with the body of his son Willie, who had died in the White House in 1862 at the age of eleven.

COURTESY OF THE CHICAGO HISTORICAL SOCIETY. ICHI-29348.

Below: Illinois' fifth capitol building was built in 1853 at a cost of $260,000.

COURTESY OF THE SANGAMON VALLEY COLLECTION AT LINCOLN LIBRARY, SPRINGFIELD.

grain-marketing location, was developing into the world's most influential exchange for buying and selling grain delivery contracts as well as treasury notes and municipal bonds. The Chicago Produce Exchange became a marketplace for butter, eggs, poultry, and other farm products. Early in the twentieth century, part of the Produce Exchange would become the Chicago Mercantile Exchange, a rival to the Board of Trade in futures and options on world currencies.

Chicago also became a center for the lumber industry. Timber floated on enormous rafts from Michigan and Wisconsin forests was transported from the city on waterways and railroads to destinations in all directions for mill work, furniture, and other wood products.

On Christmas Day in 1865, the half-square-mile Chicago Union Stockyard was opened, expanding the city's meat-packing industry that was already the largest in the world. Every day thousands of hogs, sheep, and cattle were slaughtered at the stockyards, which over the next several decades would employ thousands of Irish, German, Polish, Hungarian, Czech, Yugoslav, and Lithuanian immigrants. In 1867, George M. Pullman founded the Pullman Palace Car Company, manufacturing railroad sleeping cars.

With expanding educational opportunities, elementary and high school attendance increased significantly. Members of religious denominations, primarily Catholic and German Lutherans, established parochial schools throughout Illinois, and the state's superintendent of public instruction, Newton Bateman, helped prepare legislation to create a national bureau of education.

In 1867 the General Assembly established the land-grant Illinois Industrial University at Champaign-Urbana, which in 1885 was renamed the University of Illinois. In Carbondale, Southern Illinois Normal University was founded in 1870 as a small teachers' college with emphasis on classical subjects. Illinois State Normal University geologist John Wesley Powell, surveyor of the Rocky Mountain region, became director of the United States Geological Survey.

In 1868, Ulysses S. Grant of Galena, hero of the Civil War, was nominated by the

Republican party and elected president of the United States. He named fellow Galenans John A. Rawlins as secretary of war and Elihu Washburn as secretary of state, then minister to France. Grant chose David Davis of Bloomington as an associate justice of the U.S. Supreme Court.

During five months in 1869 and 1870, Illinois constitutional convention delegates approved a longer and more detailed document than the 1848 constitution, signifying the growth and complexity of state needs. The many changes included elimination of racial distinctions in voting, on jury panels, in schools, and in the state militia. The new constitution also provided legislative power to regulate railroads as "public highways."

By then nearly every town in Illinois supported at least one newspaper, as the state grew not only in population and wealth but also in intellectual and commercial interests. "Our people are studying more attentively," wrote Governor Oglesby in 1869, "the intimate and profitable relations between agriculture and manufactures. To secure the wealth each produces, the plow, the forge, and the spindle ought to dwell together on the same prairie. Capital is steadily seeking investment in our State, and in a few years this new interest will make us what we ought to be—a manufacturing as well as an agricultural people."

✧

Northwestern University in Chicago officially opened on November 5, 1855, with the first building, Old College, completed. Today the school is a major research university with lakefront campuses in both Chicago and Evanston.

Chapter VI

The golden age of the small town was the last quarter of the nineteenth century, a time when rural and metropolitan populations were much more in balance than today. The earlier struggle for existence, typified at New Salem, was over and the automobile had not yet ended rural isolation and accelerated the rush to the cities. During this brief period, small towns were self-sustaining places whose residents did not have to venture far from their front doors for most of the necessities of life.

- David Buisseret, *Historic Illinois from the Air*

While the state's population growth between 1860 and 1870 represented a 50 percent gain, to 2.5 million, Chicago nearly tripled in size, to 300,000, the foreign-born numbering nearly half of its residents. Chicago led the nation in receiving, processing, and marketing grain, beef, pork, and lumber, while her factories produced farm implements, wagons, and iron works. Populations of smaller cities had also grown in the 1860s, as Quincy outranked Peoria, and the number of Springfield residents increased to more than seventeen thousand.

During the 1870s, however, the population increase slowed considerably, as Illinois was still an agricultural state. Improvements in farm machinery, along with DeKalb farmer Joseph F. Glidden's design of an inexpensive "barbed" wire for fencing pastures and crops, increased productivity as well as land values. In the western United States, cattle ranchers used the new fencing to convert open ranges into pastures. "Barbed wire," wrote historian Robert P. Howard, "was credited with doing more for the West than the long rifle and covered wagon."

For transporting agricultural and industrial freight, railroads began superseding river vessels. Every day more than four hundred trains arrived in or departed from Chicago—a bustling marketplace for transporting passengers and goods between the east coast and the Great Plains.

Chicago's continuing growth was interrupted, however, in the drought autumn of 1871, when the Great Chicago Fire destroyed nearly three square miles of the central city. An estimated 300 people died, and 100,000 residents, about a third of the city's population, were left homeless. The fire consumed the entire business district, along with mansions and cottages. The Chicago Historical Society lost all of its holdings, including an original of Lincoln's Emancipation Proclamation.

Food, clothing, and generous monetary contributions helped Chicagoans recover—as did the optimism and determination of city leaders. Businesses reopened within an amazingly brief period, while architects began designing a new downtown that would transform burned-out residential sections into a center for commerce and culture. After the General Assembly passed legislation in 1872 allowing municipalities to establish tax-supported libraries, British citizens organized the English Book Donation drive, contributing more than eight thousand volumes to help Chicagoans establish a downtown public library.

In the early 1870s, farmers throughout the state began forming Grange chapters of the national Order of the Patrons of Husbandry, an organization to provide members with "social life…and broader social vision." The Grangers operated cooperative stores in about half of the state's counties, with goods at wholesale prices. Chicagoan Aaron Montgomery Ward, a traveling dry-goods salesman, established a mail-order firm as a Grange supply house, later developing it into one of the world's largest catalog and retail firms. Chicago entrepreneurs Richard W. Sears and Alvah Roebuck began a catalog business offering clothing, furniture, household items, musical instruments, and even house plans and materials.

✧

The opening of the new canal after reversing the current of the Chicago River.
COURTESY OF THE CHICAGO HISTORICAL SOCIETY. ENGRAVING; AUGUST 16, 1871; ICHI-05836

The nonpartisan Grange soon turned to political activism, in 1874 electing nine independent state legislative candidates. Opposing bills that favored the giant railroads, Grangers were instrumental in the U.S. Supreme Court *Munn v. Illinois* decision that confirmed a state's regulatory authority over railroads as public-service corporations. By the late 1870s, however, the Granger movement had lost influence as a viable political entity, and members returned to social and instructional programs.

Crop yields and land values increased following the completion of levees along river banks, particularly the Sny Island Levee on the Mississippi in Adams, Pike, and Calhoun counties. The 1870 state Constitution provided for the formation of drainage districts, and in 1878 the General Assembly authorized the districts to tax residents for levee construction, drainage improvements, and flood control. By the 1880s, district taxation funded extensive systems of levees, drains, and ditches, improving swamplands and bottomlands for cultivation.

Beginning in the 1870s, immigrants arrived in Illinois in ever-increasing numbers, still primarily from Germany and Ireland, but large numbers also came from Bohemia, Poland, Greece, Sweden, and Norway. Most settled in Chicago—which grew to a population of 1.7 million by the end of the century—and in the coal mining towns of central and southern Illinois. Many Europeans in Chicago, according to the *Tribune*, found employment as tailors, blacksmiths, and plumbers, as well as rolling-mill and packinghouse workers.

Members of these ethnic and nationality groups established organizations through which members influenced their communities. Polish-Americans organized building and loan associations, fraternal groups, and parochial schools. Greeks sponsored after-school programs and church schools, where students developed language fluency. Chicago Jews, mainly from Germany and Russia, hosted night schools, where new arrivals learned English, American history, and government. Jewish congregations also responded to social needs—in 1889 founding Michael Reese Hospital, now one of the nation's best equipped medical facilities.

The state's black population had increased three-fold between 1860 and 1870, numbering nearly twenty-nine thousand. Generally unaccepted in the regular work force, blacks served primarily as domestic servants and unskilled laborers. A few were employed as agricultural laborers, or in laundries, and fewer still in the professions or in skilled labor.

Yet in 1871, voters of Cook County elected Chicagoan John Jones to the board of commissioners, the first black to hold elective office in Illinois. Three years later Governor John A. Beveridge appointed John J. Bird, the elected police magistrate at Cairo, a trustee of the state industrial university. Chicago teacher John W. E. Thomas, a former slave and an

activist for repeal of the repressive black laws, was elected in 1876 the first black state representative. African-American surgeon Daniel Hale Williams established Provident Hospital in Chicago in 1891, the nation's first interracial hospital and the first training school for black doctors and nurses.

As the economy shifted from rural and agricultural to urban and industrial, increasing numbers of women joined the work force. By the turn of the century one of every four Chicago women was employed, primarily as domestic servants, in the garment industry, or as clerks and stenographers. Female teachers in Illinois outnumbered men at the elementary and secondary levels, but few taught in colleges or universities.

Chicago feminist Mary Livermore organized and chaired the state's first women's suffrage convention. Members of the Illinois Equal Suffrage Association, formed at the 1869 convention, lobbied successfully for a bill that secured women's wages to their own use. Livermore later won election as the first national president of the Association for the Advancement of Women. In 1874, Frances Willard, president of the Evanston College for Ladies, founded the Women's Christian Temperance Union, advocating both temperance education and woman suffrage. Four years later she became national WCTU

president, then president of the National Council of Women.

Bell Telephone Company of Illinois began operations in Chicago in 1878, and within a

year 450 businesses and five homes were connected to the service. "The telephone is superseding the telegraph," reported the *Chicago Evening Journal*; "the use of the telephone for short distances is likely to become general." By 1890 the number of telephone subscribers in the state reached nearly eight thousand and at the turn of the century would approach thirty-five thousand.

In the small railroad town of Dwight, some eighty miles southwest of Chicago, Civil War physician Leslie E. Keeley in 1879 opened the first medical institution for the treatment of alcoholism as a disease. With his partner, Irish immigrant chemist John R. Oughton, they administered "double chloride of gold" injections to alcohol-dependent patients. By 1892, twenty daily trains carried passengers to or from Dwight, and by the turn of the century, franchised Keeley Institutes operated in every state and many foreign countries. Former patients formed Keeley League clubs, which served as prototypes for the later Alcoholics Anonymous organization.

While in 1870 valuation of the state's manufactured goods nearly equaled that of agricultural commodities, by 1880 the value of factory and workshop products was larger. Chicago dominated the state's commerce and

industry, although downstate cities also supported industrial plants with sizeable workforces. In Peoria, centrally located in a fertile agricultural region, several railroads distributed grain and coal, along with manufactured products. Peoria was home to fourteen distilleries and eight breweries, agricultural implement plants, and packinghouses. In southern Illinois, East St. Louis ranked third behind Chicago and Peoria in grain storage and marketing.

Springfield's industries included foundries, railroad shops, boiler and iron works, and several coal mines. Horse-drawn street railways provided local transportation, with gaslights illuminating the central streets. After deeming the state capitol too small for the expanding government services, legislators approved construction of a much larger statehouse. The current capitol was completed in 1888, at a cost of $4.5 million.

Under provisions of the 1870 constitution, Kentucky-born Republican Shelby M. Cullom in 1880 became the first governor elected to a successive term. He resigned that office to serve as a nationally known United States senator—a position he held for thirty years—chairing the Interstate Commerce Commission and then the Committee on Foreign Relations.

The constitution also mandated tax-supported common schools, and in 1872 legislators authorized the establishment of township high schools. The state's first compulsory attendance law, in 1883, required children between the ages of eight and fourteen to attend school for twelve weeks a year, and 1889 legislation specified that children to age twelve in both public and parochial schools be taught reading, writing, arithmetic, history, and geography. Regarding blacks, the General Assembly passed legislation for desegregating public schools in 1874, then in 1885 prohibited discrimination on railroads and streetcars and in places of public accommodation and entertainment.

Industrial over-expansion and speculative railroad ventures led in 1873 to financial depression and the nation's first major labor-capital confrontation. For a decade laborers had been agitating for improved wages and working conditions, even forming small unions. In Belleville in 1861, coal workers organized the short-lived American Miners' Association, which, according to a labor historian, "may justly claim to have initiated the modern labor movement in the United States."

With forty percent unemployment in Chicago, workers began resorting to strikes

✧

The textile industry was a major source of revenue for Illinois as evidenced by Springfield Woolen Mills' seventy-eight years of continuous operation.

and other disturbances. In 1874 alone, Chicago police arrested twenty-five thousand men, mostly unemployed and mostly for minor offenses. In response to statewide labor unrest, the General Assembly in 1877 approved a militia, officially known as the Illinois National Guard, and provided funding for a well-trained and armed force.

That summer railroad managers across the country slashed workers' wages, precipitating strikes in the eastern states that spread westward in violence and intensity. In Illinois agitation began in East St. Louis, where unemployed men in other occupations, especially coal miners, joined the striking railroad workers. Bitter labor-management confrontations led to National Guard mobilization not only in East St. Louis, but also in Peoria, Galesburg, Decatur, Braidwood, and LaSalle.

As the depression continued, a group of German immigrants in Chicago began advocating revolution and political assassination. Socialist newspaper editors Albert R. Parsons and August Spies complained of "unjust" employers. At the huge McCormick reaper plant on Chicago's west side, mobs of workers fought police and the militia, resulting in some thirty-five deaths and three hundred arrests.

The economy stabilized in the early 1880s but slumped again between 1884 and 1886. Of more than a thousand strikes in Illinois, about half ended with worker concessions. At the McCormick plant, managers refused labor demands, and in February 1886, ordered a general lockout. Sporadic clashes occurred over the next several weeks, and on May 3, police killed two McCormick workers and injured others. Radical editor Spies contended that if the locked-out men had brought "good weapons and a single dynamite bomb, not one of the murderers would have escaped his well-deserved fate."

The next day Spies and Samuel Fielden, an English-born teamster turned anarchist, rallied nearly fifteen hundred workers and sympathizers at the Haymarket Square produce market, about a half mile from the McCormick plant. As police attempted to disperse the crowd, someone threw a bomb at the officers. In the ensuing gunfire, eight policemen were killed and nearly sixty wounded.

Chicago erupted in anti-foreign and anti-labor outrage. Although the bomb thrower was never identified, of the many arrested, eight, including Spies and Parsons, were charged with murder and conspiracy. In a nearly two-month trial that drew national attention, all eight were convicted—seven sentenced to death by hanging and another to a fifteen-year prison term. Parsons, the only native-born defendant, had left the meeting with his wife and children before the bomb was thrown.

The verdict won wide acclaim, although Governor Richard Oglesby commuted to life

imprisonment the sentences of two of the condemned men. Another committed suicide, and the other four, including Parsons and Spies, were hanged for the alleged crimes.

Chicagoans continued dominating the meat-packing industry, the stockyards filled "with so many cattle as no one had ever dreamed existed in the world," noted one writer. In the 1870s, meatpackers Gustavus Swift and Philip D. Armour began operating refrigerated railroad cars, allowing shipments to all parts of the country, and by the mid-1880s the major packers were also exporters, primarily to German, French, and British markets. In 1893 both Swift and Armour expanded processing capacity with plants at National City, near East St. Louis.

In Chicago commerce, real estate speculator Potter Palmer erected the opulent Palmer House Hotel and developed State Street into the city's merchandising district. Marshall Field, whose dry goods building had been destroyed by the 1871 fire, added a grand store to State Street.

Newly developed mass-production processes provided quality, high-tensile steel materials for building, bridge, and rail construction. In Chicago, the world's first steel-framed skyscraper, the ten-story Home Insurance Building designed by William Le Baron Jenney, was constructed in 1885 at LaSalle and Adams streets. Daniel Burnham and John Wellborn Root's sixteen-

story Monadnock Building on West Jackson Boulevard opened in 1891 as the city's tallest office building. Louis Sullivan and his engineering partner Dankmar Adler produced more than a hundred structures, including in 1889 the renowned Auditorium Theater at Michigan Avenue and Congress Street. Sullivan later designed the ornate twelve-story Carson Pirie Scott and Company retail store on State Street.

Although rail lines carried most of Illinois' agricultural and industrial commerce, river traffic continued as well. Paralleling the route

✧

Above: After a bomb exploded during a labor protest at Haymarket Square, on May 4, 1886, eight officers were reported dead and sixty injured. It was later found that most of the injuries were actually caused by their own bullets as they blindly fired during the blast.

Below: The Palmer House grand dining room.

of the Illinois and Michigan Canal, the new $100-million Chicago Sanitary and Ship Canal reversed the flow of the Chicago River to limit contamination of the lake water supply and linked the south fork with the Illinois River waterway system.

In 1890, Illinois ranked behind only New York and Pennsylvania as a manufacturing center. Still, with more than a quarter-million farms at the turn of the century, agriculture remained the state's most populous industry. The leading downstate counties in gross value of flouring-mill products were Peoria, St. Clair, Adams, and Madison, while Rock Island County became a center for lumber products as well as farm implements.

The cities of Belleville, East St. Louis, Alton, Edwardsville, and Granite City contributed foundry products, a growing iron and steel industry, glass making, and brewing, along with slaughtering and meat-packing. In Kane County, Elgin became a center for dairy products, printing and publishing, and watch-making. Aurora had a large foundry and machine shop concentration and was a major manufacturer of railroad cars. Industrial output in Rockford, Winnebago County, included furniture, hosiery and clothing, and agricultural implements.

Coal was also becoming a more important commodity, the state geologist noting in 1886 that the abundance of soft bituminous coal would propel the state into the industrial forefront. The largest coal-producing counties were St. Clair, Sangamon, Vermilion, Madison, Macoupin, and LaSalle, each by the 1890s mining more than a million tons annually.

The industrial growth of cities led to development of national organizations, including the Young Men's Christian Association, offering educational programs and recreational activities. In Chicago in 1889, social reformer Jane Addams and her college friend Ellen Gates Starr founded Hull House, a community service project in an industrial west-side Chicago neighborhood. Helping poor, especially immigrant, families, the settlement-house women provided educational programs and advocated political reform, improved city services, and child protection measures.

"There were no laws regulating the sweatshop industries," Addams explained. "We found children of all ages going to work whenever it suited the convenience of their parents, and many of them coming to grief from premature labor. We found many newly imported Italians and others working in sweatshops for phenomenally low wages, with no regulations as to the sanitary conditions under which they were working."

Over the next two decades, Hull House staff and volunteers built Chicago's first playground and helped Mary M. Bartleme, public guardian of Cook County, develop the nation's first juvenile court. Their efforts resulted in landmark child-labor and workshop legislation, along with regulated factory inspections. Florence Kelley of Hull House was appointed the state's first factory inspector, while her associate Julia Lathrop, a Rockford native and Vassar graduate, would become the first director of the State Board of Charities and later head a new federal children's bureau. Grace Abbott succeeded Lathrop in the state position, and her sister Edith Abbott, a University of Chicago dean, became superintendent of the League for the Protection of Immigrants.

During the half-century of Republican ascendancy in Illinois, the party seemingly grew more conservative, while the Democrats, with a large urban component, had in some respects become more progressive. With support from

labor organizations and rural populists, Cook County judge John Peter Altgeld won the 1892 gubernatorial race, and fellow Democrat Adlai Ewing Stevenson, a former Bloomington congressman, was elected U.S. vice-president on the ticket with Grover Cleveland. Democrats now controlled the political systems in both Washington and Illinois.

Reading the trial and appeal records from the 1886 Haymarket Riot, Altgeld determined that prosecutors did not prove any direct connection between the bombing and the anarchists. He granted pardons to the three surviving men, a highly unpopular decision that contributed to ending the one-term governor's public career.

By mid-1892, the new industrial economy was suffering a serious recession. Yet the following May, President Cleveland opened the World's Columbian Exposition in Chicago, a patriotic four hundredth anniversary commemoration of the discovery of America. Nearly every state and forty-six foreign nations participated in the six-month cultural and entertainment fair, located on six hundred south-side acres near Lake Michigan. Exhibitors introduced 27.5 million visitors to such consumer products as Cream of Wheat and Shredded Wheat cereals, carbonated soda, and hamburgers, as well as the world's first Ferris Wheel, a gargantuan structure holding forty passengers in each of thirty-six cars.

Within days of the Fair's opening, however, securities prices fell dramatically, generating a financial panic. Throughout the nation and in Illinois, banks and businesses failed, and farm-product prices plummeted, as did factory and mine production. By the end of the year, the country was in the throes of a four-year depression, one of the worst in American history.

Probably in no state were the effects more far reaching than in Illinois, and certainly no city suffered more than Chicago. Many of the workers hired for the World's Fair were left without employment or prospects; by the winter of 1893 more than two hundred thousand

✧

Above: An architectural sketch of the Hall of Honor of the proposed 1893 World's Columbian Exposition looking east toward Lake Michigan.

Below: Midway Plaisance of the Columbian Exposition looking east toward the world's first Ferris Wheel.

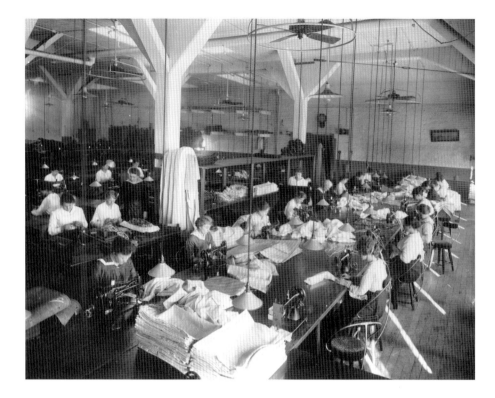

Chicagoans were jobless. Miners throughout the state saw their wages reduced to an average of $12 a month. Some three hundred miners in the LaSalle County town of Spring Valley offered themselves in servitude in return for shelter, food, and clothing. The Illinois National Guard was mobilized nine times in the spring of 1894 to control sporadic trouble at the mines.

As sales of Pullman Palace cars slumped, managers reduced wages as much as twenty-five percent. Rents at George Pullman's company town, however, were not lowered; paymasters subtracted the rent payments from

workers' shrinking paychecks. Members of an employee committee seeking to meet with Pullman were fired. In desperation, some four thousand Pullman workers joined the new American Railway Union, led by former Indiana legislator and labor advocate Eugene V. Debs.

During the summer of 1894 and culminating two decades of labor unrest in Illinois, the ARU's 150,000 members refused to handle trains bearing Pullman cars or equipment. Within a few days, more than 124,000 workers left their jobs, and strikers soon shut down the rail system from Chicago to the west coast. The General Managers Association, representing 24 railroads serving Chicago, refused to negotiate with union representatives and instead hired 3,600 federal deputy marshals to break the strike.

President Cleveland issued a sweeping injunction against the ARU, charging "interference with interstate commerce and postal service," but strikers ignored the injunction. He then ordered federal troops to Chicago, where looting mobs destroyed and stole railroad property, causing $80 million in property and wage losses.

The strike and the ARU collapsed. Many newspapers, without foundation, blamed immigrant workers for the destruction. "The names of most of the men wounded in the Chicago riots are Polish puzzles," opined Springfield's *Illinois State Register*. "It is safe to say that not one of them has sufficient intelligence to run a railroad." For violating the injunction, Debs and other union officials were convicted of contempt of court—a decision upheld by the U.S. Supreme Court.

Labor strife continued throughout the state. Worker complaints of low pay were exacerbated by frequent lockouts and the hiring of strikebreakers, including blacks from the south. Miners' antagonism led in 1890 to their forming the United Mine Workers of America. In Spring Valley, one miner was killed and several injured in an 1895 riot involving whites and blacks. Two years later, with business conditions improving and coal demand increasing, some forty thousand miners walked off the job. Within weeks, owners conceded a twenty percent pay increase.

The union was tested again in 1898 at mines in Virden and Pana, south of Springfield. The operators imported black laborers to both towns, and violence at Virden resulted in the deaths of twelve miners and guards. Republican Governor John R. Tanner publicly supported the workers: "These avaricious mine owners who have so far forgotten their duty to society as to bring this blot upon the fair name of our state have gone far enough." He sent the militia to restore order and prevent the importing of additional strikebreakers.

State UMW president John Mitchell of Spring Valley was elected national president in 1899, after winning a strike settlement in Mount Olive that included an eight-hour workday and six-day work week. Wages remained low, however, for the dangerous work, and newly arriving Slavic and Italian immigrants competed for jobs with Welsh, Irish, English and Scotch miners.

The long depression ended in 1898, with the return of decade-long economic prosperity and increases in union membership. Despite strong resistance by employers, the American Federation of Labor and the United Mine Workers won state laws for worker protection, including a prohibition on child labor in mines and restrictions in factory and sweatshop jobs.

Even as Illinois struggled with labor and economic woes, educational and cultural advancements contributed to strengthening the new industrial state. During the 1890s legislators established three state-supported teacher-training colleges: Eastern Illinois Normal at Charleston, Northern Illinois Normal at DeKalb, and Western Illinois Normal at Macomb. New York philanthropist John D. Rockefeller generously contributed to establishing the University of Chicago, whose founding president, William Rainey Harper, was a Rockefeller friend. "The good Lord gave me the money," Rockefeller stated, "and how could I withhold it from Chicago?" The new school soon ranked among the nation's preeminent educational institutions.

The Chicago Symphony Orchestra, founded in 1891, performed twice-weekly concerts at the Auditorium Theater. The Art Institute of Chicago's building on Michigan Avenue was completed in 1892, the Field Museum of Natural History in 1893, and the Chicago Public Library in 1895. Four years later, the Illinois State Historical Society was organized at Springfield, to promote interest in the state's history and to support programs of the State Historical Library, established in 1889. And throughout the state, grants from industrialist Andrew Carnegie funded more than one hundred libraries, with local communities, many assisted by women's, immigrant, and literary societies providing the building sites and maintenance funding.

By the close of the century, Illinois was the nation's third most powerful industrial state. Twenty-four towns had grown to populations of more than 10,000. In 1896, London journalist George W. Steevens described Chicago, the nation's second largest city, as "the most American" of American cities, "the great mart which gathers up with one hand the corn and cattle of the West and deals out with the other the merchandise of the East."

Opposite, top: Although George Pullman felt that he was improving the lives of his employees at Pullman Works by providing housing, shopping, and entertainment in the company town, workers felt they were living in slave-like conditions. When Pullman shop employees took a stand against wage cuts and oppressive labor practices, it led to a nationwide boycott of trains carrying Pullman cars.

COURTESY OF THE CHICAGO HISTORICAL SOCIETY. ORIGINAL PULLMAN NEGATIVE. PHOTOGRAPH; ICHI-19682.

Opposite, bottom: The Pullman strike of 1894 resulted in dozens of railroad cars burned on side tracks. This view shows the results of labor violence near Burnside crossing and 104th Street.

COURTESY OF THE CHICAGO HISTORICAL SOCIETY. ICHI-04899.

Below: On October 12, 1898, Virden, Illinois, was the site of a bloody battle between mine guards and miners that left eight miners and four guards dead.

COURTESY OF THE SANGAMON VALLEY COLLECTION AT LINCOLN LIBRARY, SPRINGFIELD.

CHAPTER VII

INDUSTRIALIZATION & MODERNIZATION, 1900-1930

Illinois, like the United States as a whole, entered the twentieth century with exuberant confidence. The progress that had characterized the years since the Civil War would continue and at an ever faster rate: that few doubted. Both the state at large and Chicago would grow in population; farms and mines would produce in ever-increasing abundance; factory output would mount to unpredictable figures....

Illinois farms kept the state in first place in agricultural production. In spite of strikes and labor troubles, coal output increased. Factories turned out even larger quantities of goods, and added new products in response to advancing technology.

- Paul Angle, *Prairie State*

With the new century came anticipation of a modern Illinois, including additional laws for protection of laborers, women, and children. The 1900 federal census indicated that Illinois was now an urban state; for the first time, more than half of its five million population lived in towns or cities.

Illinois was also becoming a national political force. Salem native William Jennings Bryan in 1896 won the first of three Democratic presidential nominations, although losing twice to William McKinley and then to William Howard Taft. In 1912, President Woodrow Wilson chose Bryan as the U.S. secretary of state. Conservative Danville Republican Joseph G. Cannon, first elected to the House of Representatives in 1872, became speaker of the House in 1903, holding the position for four successive terms.

In agriculture, mechanization advances now included threshers and motorized tractors. International Harvester Company, formed from a merger of McCormick and other implement firms, made agricultural equipment in Chicago and in Rock Island. Deere & Company in Moline, by then the world's largest plow manufacturer, also began producing mechanized equipment, as did Holt Manufacturing Company in Peoria. Decatur manufacturer A. E. Staley opened the nation's first commercial soybean-processing plant, while three Illinois farmers, Eugene Funk of Bloomington, C. L. Gunn of DeKalb, and Lester Pfister of El Paso developed hybrid seeds that resulted in substantially increased crop yields—among the most significant agricultural advances of the twentieth century.

Coal mining in the early 1900s provided employment for some 36,000 workers. A 1904 law prohibited child labor in mines, and after a disastrous 1909 fire killed 259 men in the Bureau County mine at Cherry, the General Assembly enacted safety and liability legislation that evolved into the Illinois Workmen's Compensation Act. In 1920, former miner John L. Lewis of Springfield began a forty-year tenure as national United Mine Workers president.

The General Assembly in 1913 granted women the right to vote in presidential elections. "In voting for the suffrage measure," wrote suffragist Grace Wilbur Trout, those legislators "made themselves forever great—they gave Illinois a place in history no other state can ever fill, for Illinois was the first state east of the Mississippi and the first state even bordering the great father of waters, to break down the conservatism of the great Middle West and give suffrage to its women. . . . New York women never could have won their great suffrage victory in 1917 if Illinois had not first opened the door in 1913."

For blacks, however, civil and political rights were still elusive. In Springfield in August 1908, a white woman's false claim of being raped by a black man resulted in an infamous race riot. Two blacks were lynched, 4 whites were killed, and 79 others injured. Five thousand

William Jennings Bryan (with coat on arm) and Mrs. Bryan standing with a group of people, including Chicago Mayor Edward Dunne, 1906.

militiamen patrolled streets of the capital city to restore order.

News of the riot spread across the country and throughout the world. In New York, influential national leaders, including Jane Addams and black scholar W. E. B. DuBois, helped organize the National Association for the Advancement of Colored People in 1910. Chicagoans established the first NAACP branch, promoting legal and political rights for blacks.

By then, the state was becoming a literary and cultural center, with such writers as Edgar Lee Masters, Carl Sandburg, Floyd Dell, Theodore Dreiser, and Harriet Monroe. Springfield poet Vachel Lindsay received his first public recognition in Monroe's *Poetry* magazine.

In architecture, Frank Lloyd Wright, Louis Sullivan's chief assistant, designed horizontal "prairie school" residences, which he described as a "city man's country home on the prairie." Among Wright structures that became architectural landmarks are Unity Temple in Oak Park and the elegant Dana-Thomas House in Springfield. Chicago sculptor Lorado Taft created works around the world, including the Alma Mater statue at the University of Illinois and one of the Sauk warrior Black Hawk, which overlooks the Rock River near Oregon.

In 1910 Chicago newspaper publisher W. D. Boyce incorporated the Boy Scouts of America, with support from the organization's British founder, Lord Baden-Powell. Within six years, eight thousand youngsters and their leaders established scout troops in cities and towns throughout the country. Boyce in 1915 founded and for ten years funded the Lone Scouts of America, a similar organization for boys on farms and in rural areas. Then, citing his inability to financially sustain the Lone Scouts, he arranged for its merger with the Boy Scouts of America.

At the federal level, reforms in national and state banking regulations—the most extensive since the administration of President Andrew Jackson—led in 1913 to a central banking plan known as the Federal Reserve System. Of the twelve regional districts, the Federal Reserve Bank in Chicago continues to serve the financial institutions in the upper Midwest, while the St. Louis, Missouri, Federal Reserve Bank serves those in southern Illinois.

In 1917, newly elected Governor Frank O. Lowden convinced the Illinois General Assembly to approve a long-needed governmental reorganization that would have national influence. The Civil Administrative Code reduced a myriad of state agencies, boards, and commissions into nine departments, each headed by a director in the

governor's cabinet. That centralized plan remains in effect today, although the number of agencies has again increased substantially.

The 1918 centennial of Illinois statehood coincided with America's involvement in world war—one that Britain and France had been waging since 1914 against Germany. The German-born population of Illinois numbered more than three hundred thousand, larger than in any other state. Twenty-five German-American Chicagoans urged President Wilson against allying with Britain and France, while Jane Addams, chairman of the new Woman's Peace party, won support from prominent businessmen in opposing the war on humanitarian and moral grounds. Illinois representatives provided five of the fifty votes against a congressional declaration of war.

But when the Democratic president broke off diplomatic relations with Germany, Republican Governor Lowden and Illinois legislators pledged unanimous support of the national administration. The Illinois National Guard was mustered into federal service, while drafted men from northern Illinois and southern Wisconsin trained at Camp Grant, near Rockford. Southern Illinois draftees were sent to Camp Zachary Taylor at Louisville, Kentucky. Fort Sheridan, built near Chicago during the 1880s labor unrest, became an officers' training camp and then a hospital. The Great Lakes Naval Training Station, opened in 1904 in Lake County, provided facilities for fifty thousand recruits, while Scott Field near Belleville and Chanute

Field at Rantoul housed aviation bases and flight schools.

By enlistment and conscription, Illinois sent more than 350,000 men to the war. Munitions and other war materials comprised a third of the state's 1918 industrial production. Farmers received draft deferments in order to increase food production, and teenaged boys obtained education credits for agricultural work.

East St. Louis, growing faster than any other Illinois city in the decade, provided aluminum and animal-feed products for the war effort. A worker shortage caused factory managers to encourage the migration to East St. Louis of some ten thousand Southern blacks. Those new arrivals aggravated existing racial tensions by moving into already overcrowded slums and taking jobs at lower wages than those paid to white workers. In 1917, after several whites aimed gunfire at black homes, blacks retaliated by killing two white policemen. In the next twenty-four hours, at least thirty-nine blacks and nine whites died in riots; forty freight cars and 250 buildings were burned.

In Chicago, the black population more than doubled between 1910 and 1920, those 100,000 residing primarily in an eight-square-mile area on the south side, with some moving into white neighborhoods. Racial friction escalated in the summer of 1919, and

✧

Above: A wealthy publisher and author, W. D. Boyce traveled the world in search of adventure. He used the skills and knowledge he gained on his travels to incorporate the Boy Scouts of America.

COURTESY OF THE ILLINOIS STATE HISTORICAL SOCIETY

Below: 131st Infantry "doughboys" charge with bayonets fixed during drills at Camp Logan, near Zion, Illinois.

COURTESY OF THE CHICAGO HISTORICAL SOCIETY.
CHICAGO DAILY NEWS. GLASS NEGATIVE; 1916; DN-0087972

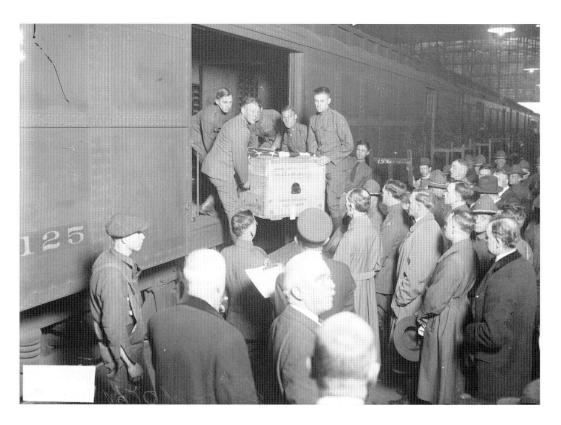

in a two-week series of street fights, twenty-three blacks and fifteen whites were killed. Hundreds more were injured, with more than a thousand, mostly black, left homeless from fires and riots. "It was the nation's worst race war," according to historian John Hope Franklin, "and shocked even the most indifferent persons into a realization that interracial conflicts in the United States had reached a serious stage."

Despite discrimination and violence, black migration into Illinois continued. The influential African-American newspaper *Chicago Defender* carried articles about the north's relative freedoms and economic opportunities. Between 1920 and 1930 Chicago blacks increased from 4.1 percent to 6.9 percent of the population. Black politician Edward H. Morris of Cook County won a legislative seat in 1890 and 1902, attorney William L. Martin in 1898, and John G. Jones in 1900, after which the number of blacks in politics grew steadily. In 1928 Chicago alderman Oscar DePriest would become the first northern black in the U.S. Congress.

For nearly three decades, women could cast ballots for some offices, but in June 1919, Illinois ratified the Nineteenth Amendment for full women's suffrage. Then in 1922, Republican Lottie Holman O'Neill of Downers Grove won election as the first woman state legislator, serving for thirty-eight years.

As Illinois expanded its transportation network, only Calhoun County, bordering the Mississippi, lacked a rail line in 1920. Beginning in 1899 with the St. Louis, Belleville, & Suburban Railway Company, electric interurbans provided service between towns and rural areas. Within ten years, more than a thousand miles of electric rail crisscrossed the state.

Champaign banker William Brown McKinley developed a utility empire that included electric and gas companies and the Illinois Traction System, an interurban line comprising some four hundred miles of track. He also operated streetcar lines in nineteen Illinois cities, and in 1910 completed the McKinley Bridge across the Mississippi at St. Louis, "hailed with joy by the people of that city," according to a trade report. "It supplied improved facilities for shipments of merchandise to Illinois towns, and also afforded the opportunity for the people of these towns to make frequent shopping trips to St. Louis."

A McKinley rival, Chicagoan Samuel Insull, also operated several lines in the state, including commuter and freight service into downtown Chicago. At the peak of his success, Insull also controlled Commonweath Edison and Peoples Gas Company, supplying electricity and natural gas to the entire Chicago area.

Then as automobiles became popular and counties and townships began improving roadways, many of the interurban and streetcar lines were abandoned. Legislators approved bills requiring that automobile license revenue be expended on rural roads and bridges and allowing counties to sell bonds for state-aid roads.

The U.S. Congress in 1916 began matching state highway expenditures with federal appropriations. With a $60-million, voter-approved bond issue and the leadership of Republican Governor Lennington Small, state officials developed a paved-road system to "pull Illinois out of the mud." Within several years every county had at least one paved route, and in 1929 a three-cent motor fuel tax included one cent for secondary routes. By the following year, the state had some seventy-five hundred miles of paved road, although township roads, which served most farmers, were still primarily dirt surfaced.

The most famous road traversing Illinois was Route 66, a highway stretching from Chicago to Los Angeles, California. The Illinois portion was a north-south connection between Chicago and

East St. Louis. Route 66 linked hundreds of rural communities with larger markets.

Another emerging form of transportation was air travel. Early in the century several Illinois manufacturers provided airplanes for exhibition pilots and wealthy sportsmen. In 1918, pilots flew war-surplus planes on a mail route between New York and Chicago, and within a few years, four mail-service airlines served Chicago. Then in 1927, youthful

✧

Above: William B. McKinley at his desk, while a Republican member of the U.S. House of Representatives. McKinley gained wealth in the utility and construction industries. In 1910 he built the McKinley Bridge over the Mississippi River at St. Louis. McKinley served as a senator from March 4, 1921, until his death on December 7, 1926.

COURTESY OF THE CHICAGO HISTORICAL SOCIETY. PHOTOGRAPHIC PRINT; DN-0071783

Left: Samuel Insull, president of Commonwealth Edison Company, standing with a group of men around a table. The power company built by Insull provided electric power and natural gas to the entire Chicago metropolitan area.

COURTESY OF THE CHICAGO HISTORICAL SOCIETY. GLASS NEGATIVE; 1926; DN-0080023.

aviator Charles A. Lindbergh began daily mail-delivery flights from St. Louis, with stops in Springfield and Peoria.

Near East St. Louis, Oliver L. Parks founded a private air college for training commercial pilots, and in 1929 airports there and at Glenview became bases for civil and military planes. On Chicago's southwest side, the Municipal Airport, later renamed Midway, was dedicated in 1927—for a time it was the world's busiest commercial airport.

The 1920s saw increasing interest in sporting events, from boxing and bowling to horse racing and golf, as well as college events. Baseball became popular in the 1870s with Rockford's Forest City Nine and its star, Adrian "Cap" Anson. He then became player/manager of the new professional Chicago White Stockings of the National League, renamed the Chicago Cubs in 1902 after the Chicago White Sox became the city's American League team. In 1906 the Sox defeated the Cubs in the only World Series between the two teams. The Cubs won the 1908 Series against the Detroit Tigers, and in 1917, the White Sox defeated the New York Giants. But two years later, Sox players were implicated in the "Black Sox" scandal for throwing the Series to the Cincinnati Red Legs.

One of the era's most renowned athletes was the "galloping ghost," University of Illinois halfback Harold "Red" Grange. In 1921, football coach George Halas relocated his Decatur Staleys team to the Chicago Cubs' stadium, Wrigley Field, and renamed the team the Chicago Bears, "in honor," he said, "of the Chicago Cubs." By the 1930s, now with Grange on the team, Halas' Bears dominated professional football. They would win eight championships between 1932 and 1986. The rival Chicago Cardinals won in 1925 and again in 1947.

For the first two decades of the century, Chicago was a leader in the new motion picture industry. Essanay Studios specialized

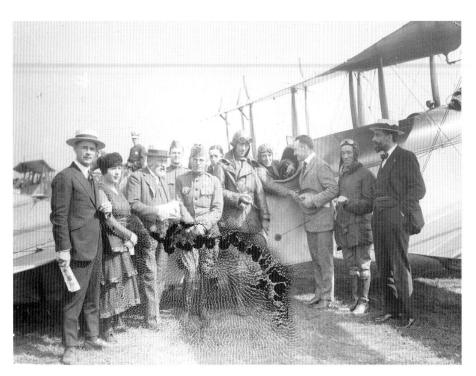

in comedies and westerns, contracting with actors Charles Chaplin, Wallace Beery, Gloria Swanson, and Francis X. Bushman. By the early 1920s, the city had twenty-three movie theaters, and in downstate towns, entrepreneurs built smaller versions of big-city theaters, including their opulent decors.

Illinois radio began in 1921, when Chicago station KYW broadcast a program of opera music. Two years later, the *Chicago Tribune*, the "World's Greatest Newspaper," purchased the fledgling WDAP station and changed the call letters to WGN. The *Tribune*'s innovative publisher, Robert R. McCormick, penned his mother: "I have written to arrange to have an operator come to your room with a radio set and give you an exhibition. I don't think you will want to keep one, but you cannot help being thrilled at the little box that picks sounds from the air."

Sears, Roebuck, the "World's Largest Store," owned Chicago station WLS, hosting the popular Saturday evening *National Barn Dance*, along with drama, variety, and public affairs programs. Soon radio stations were operated in cities and towns throughout the state, and by 1929, the majority of Illinois families owned at least one set. Among radio manufacturers in the state were Zenith Radio Corporation, incorporated in 1923, and Motorola, in 1924.

In early 1919, Illinois joined other states in ratifying the Eighteenth Amendment, which prohibited the manufacture, sale or transportation of intoxicating liquors. During the ensuing era of national Prohibition, organized gangs in Chicago and downstate battled to control illegal alcohol sales and distribution. The number of speakeasies—"speak softly when ordering" bars and retail outlets for illicit liquor sales—increased from twelve thousand in 1922 to twenty thousand in 1926. The underground syndicates grossed millions in revenue. On St. Valentine's Day, 1929, henchmen of Chicago crime overlord Alphonse Capone gunned down seven members of a rival gang, exposing the ruthlessness of gangsterism.

Downstate bootleggers cautiously supplied customers with mostly locally produced alcohol. In far southern Illinois, gang wars

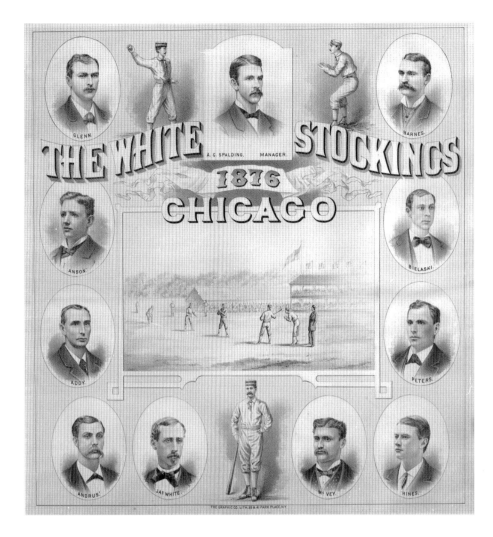

between rivals Charles Birger and the sons of Wayne County farmer Ben Shelton resulted in at least fourteen murders, including two mayors and a state highway patrolman. After Birger was hanged in 1929 for one of the shootings, the Sheltons expanded operations into other downstate areas. The gangster violence continued until 1933, when Congress enacted the Twenty-third Amendment repealing Prohibition.

Into the 1920s, Illinoisans enjoyed relative prosperity, and throughout the decade, no Democratic party candidate would win statewide office. In 1924, conservative Evanston Republican Charles Gates Dawes was elected the second vice president from Illinois, and the following year he received the Nobel Prize for Peace for the "Dawes Plan" to reorganize Germany's World War I reparations payments. Hull House founder Jane Addams, a lifelong activist for the poor and needy, in 1931 became the first American woman awarded the Nobel Prize for Peace.

CHAPTER VIII

Out of the prairie lands of Illinois, out of the swamplands of Chicago, men have created an agricultural and industrial area that is phenomenal even in this land of miracles. Chicago is the "Central Market" for Illinois and the nation. As part of Chicago's hinterland, Illinois is as essential to Chicago as Chicago is to Illinois. Together, city and state occupy a position that is unique in the United States.

- Evelyn F. Carlson, *A Great City and State; The Story of Chicago and Illinois* [1947]

A national stock market crash in October 1929, shattered the progress and seeming prosperity of the early century, leading to the Great Depression. By the end of the year, financial and real estate investors had lost more than $40 billion, followed by business failures and massive unemployment. As industrial demand fell, banks closed throughout the state. Freight revenue for the Illinois Central Railroad fell by half, and its stock price plummeted from $137 in 1930 to $5 in 1932. Illinois farm income plunged 60 percent between the late 1920s and the early 1930s.

In Chicago, the unemployed "scoured the streets and alleys for firewood and scraps of garbage," wrote historian Lloyd Wendt, "and thousands of jobless men slept under double-decked Wacker Drive and Michigan Avenue." Utilities millionaire Samuel Insull, the city's leading citizen as well as president and chief financier of the Chicago Civic Opera, watched as his corporations—which produced one-eighth of the nation's electricity and gas—fell into receivership. He would die destitute several years later.

By 1932, one-fourth of Illinois factory workers were unemployed, including 750,000 in Chicago. Other severely affected cities were Moline, Rockford, Rock Island, Danville, Quincy, and Joliet, along with southern Illinois mining counties, particularly Franklin and Williamson. Charitable volunteers and government employees operated soup kitchens, while Chicago public school teachers, facing payless paydays themselves, provided lunches for more than eleven thousand hungry students. The governor received monthly Illinois National Guard reports on threats of violence around the state.

In 1932, Democratic New York Governor Franklin D. Roosevelt defeated President Herbert Hoover, blamed by most of the nation for the Depression. To fight the desperate economic situation, Roosevelt announced a "New Deal," offering federal funds and controls on the securities industry to help banks, businesses, and railroads reopen and regain stability. Those efforts impacted Illinois industry as well as its urban and rural life.

Through Roosevelt's Rural Electrification Administration, the number of Illinois farms lighted by electricity increased from 16 percent in 1930 to 43 percent ten years later. The Civilian Conservation Corps, the Works Progress Administration, and several educational and art-related programs provided government-paid employment. More than one hundred thousand Illinois men joined the CCC, helping with construction, flood control, soil conservation, and reforestation work. Many murals painted by WPA artists hang in post offices throughout the state, and CCC projects included log lodges built at Pere Marquette and Starved Rock state parks. In all, approximately half of Illinois residents received some form of government financial assistance in the years between 1929 and 1942.

In 1933 the U.S. Army Corps of Engineers replaced the aging Illinois and Michigan Canal with the Illinois Waterway, improving the Illinois River for barge transport of coal, oil, and other heavy commodities. On the Mississippi River, the Corps of Engineers began a multi-year project to construct a series of locks and dams, described as the "engineering eighth wonder." Some thirteen

✧

Placed in charge of the Manhattan Project at the University of Chicago, physicist Enrico Fermi and his team developed the first atomic pile and the first nuclear chain reaction. Today, Fermi is remembered as the "father of the atomic bomb."

thousand worked on the project during the 1930s to deepen the channel for flood control and improved river commerce.

During the summers of 1933 and 1934, Chicago hosted its second world's fair, planned in earlier prosperous times. The "Century of Progress" featured exhibits depicting social, scientific, and technological advances during the city's one-hundred-year history. Despite the continuing Depression, the two-year fair attracted thirty-nine million visitors. One feature connected with the celebration was the first professional All-Star baseball game, played at Comiskey Park, stadium of the White Sox. The sport's greatest player, Babe Ruth of the New York Yankees, starred in the 4-2 American League victory.

Another Depression-era measure was the National Labor Relations Act of 1935, guaranteeing workers the right to organize for collective bargaining. Unions struggled for recognition under the NLRA, and with the number of miners still far exceeding available work, several large, sometimes violent, strikes occurred. Scot and Welsh miners in Macoupin County suspected collusion between United Mine Workers president John L. Lewis and the state's largest mine operation, Peabody Coal Company. The dissidents formed a

second union, the Progressive Miners of America, which at its peak reported twenty thousand members. Bloody warfare erupted between the rival unions in Springfield, Christian County, and further south. Then after Lewis negotiated contracts that provided wage increases and benefits for members of both unions, the PWA eventually disbanded.

Yet, labor strife continued in other industries. In 1937, owners of several steel companies, including the massive Republic Steel in Chicago, refused to sign worker contracts. The Steel Workers Organizing Committee, a group intent on unionizing the plants, called a nationwide strike. On Memorial Day, hundreds of strikers and sympathizers marched to the Republic mill on Chicago's southeast side. About two hundred protesters began shouting and throwing rocks and bricks at nearby police, who responded with a flurry of tear gas and gunfire. In the ensuing melee ten demonstrators were killed; at least sixty marchers and forty police were injured. City officials denied charges of police brutality, but a congressional investigation later condemned the police for excessive force. Shortly after Memorial Day, the strike folded, and the steelworkers returned to their jobs. Filmed coverage of the strike reportedly brought public sympathy for the picketers and an increased acceptance of unions.

In 1937, oil had been discovered in Marion and Jefferson counties, creating a southern Illinois economic boom. Although oil and gas had been produced in the eastern part of the state since the 1890s, these new finds were in much larger and deeper reservoirs. Clay, Richland, Jasper, and Fayette counties also held deep oil zones, and by the peak year, 1940, the state's total production rose to nearly 148 million barrels. That year, near Salem in Marion County, daily production reached 259,000 barrels, and Salem became the eastern terminus of a 550-mile petroleum pipeline from Texas. In Jefferson County, 1945 production approached five million barrels, and Mount Vernon boasted of nearly three hundred "oil families." By 1949, county officials reported a ten-year crude oil yield of more than 30 million barrels, valued in excess of $50 million. For the next fifteen years, annual oil production averaged eighty million barrels, after which new finds did not hold sufficient oil to replace yields from depleted fields.

Politically, Republican domination since the 1896 elections began to wane in the late 1920s. In 1931, Czech-born Democrat Anton Cermak was elected mayor of Chicago, establishing party control that would endure in most of the state for a decade and in the city to the present time. Two years after his election, however, Cermak died in an assassination attempt on President Roosevelt.

As Cermak's replacement, the Chicago City Council approved Edward J. Kelly, chief engineer of the Chicago Sanitary District. He partnered in the mayoral position with Patrick Nash, a wealthy sewer contractor and chairman of the Cook County Democratic Central Committee. Known as the Kelly-Nash Machine, the two men centralized Chicago political influence.

As the Depression waned, threat of European war again stimulated the American economy. As early as 1938, factories throughout Illinois began making military equipment for the British and French allies. Preparing for potential war, Congress in 1940 established the first peacetime draft in U.S. history. Illinois Republican Congressman Everett M. Dirksen, a leading critic of Roosevelt's New Deal, supported the President's foreign policy and aid to the Allies. After Japanese submarines and aircraft attacked the American Navy's Pacific Fleet at Pearl Harbor, Hawaii, the United States was drawn into the two-ocean World War II.

Fort Sheridan became an Army induction center for men as well as women and later served as a prisoner-of-war camp. Other training facilities were opened at Camp Grant near Rockford and Camp Ellis near Galesburg. Chanute Field at Rantoul and Scott Field near Belleville became aeronautics-training centers. North of Chicago, the Great Lakes Naval Training Station prepared more than a

Above: Anton Cermak was the mayor of Chicago from 1931 until his death in 1933. Cermak died of gunshot wounds on March 6 during an assassination attempt on Franklin Roosevelt.

Below: Scenes like this gusher became common in southern Illinois during the late 1930s.

million sailors for active duty—nearly one-third of all Navy personnel. Abbott Hall at Northwestern University became the nation's largest midshipmen's school.

With hybrid seeds, fertilizers, insecticides, and herbicides, farmers met wartime needs for soybeans and corn. Processing plants sprang up along rail sidings, and the A. E. Staley plant in Decatur became the nation's leading soybean processor. Route 66, the shortest course from Chicago to the west coast, carried lengthy troop and supply convoys, helping facilitate the single greatest wartime mobilization in American history.

After receiving reports of atomic-bomb research in Germany, the federal government secretly assembled hundreds of scientists at the University of Chicago's Stagg Field. There, led by 1938 Nobel Prize-winning physicist Enrico Fermi, they achieved the first self-sustaining, controlled nuclear chain reaction. In 1946 the Atomic Energy Commission moved the reactor to the Argonne National Laboratory, a renowned scientific research facility on Route 66 near Lemont, along the Des Plaines River. Today the University of Chicago operates the laboratory, where nearly two thousand scientists and engineers

PANORAMA
OF
A CENTURY OF PROGRESS EXPOSITION
CHICAGO · 1933

research both military and civilian uses of nuclear energy.

African-American migration to Illinois greatly increased during the war years, especially in Chicago, where the number of blacks grew from 4.9 to 11.7 percent of the workforce. In 1942, Chicago educator James Farmer founded the Congress of Racial Equality, an interracial civil-rights organization based on non-violent resistance to segregation in public accommodations. By the 1970s, CORE would evolve from Farmer's Gandhian beliefs to a "Black Power" ideology

and eventually to "pragmatic nationalism," supporting black economic development and community self-determination.

The return of world peace in 1945 found Illinois more firmly established as a major industrial state, the chief manufacturer of radios and other electronics and moving rapidly into television production. At the University of Illinois, electrical engineer John Bardeen and two colleagues developed the transistor, beginning the technological "information age." Chicago's first television station, WBKB, started transmitting in 1943,

✧

Built for military purposes during WWII, O'Hare Airport in Chicago was appropriately named for military hero, Lieutenant Edward O'Hare, who was awarded the Congressional Medal of Honor in 1942. O'Hare International has since become the world's busiest airport.
COURTESY OF THE CHICAGO HISTORICAL SOCIETY. PHOTOGRAPH; 1960; ICHI-19581.

CHAPTER VIII

followed by other stations throughout the state. Chicagoans Burr Tillstrom and Fran Allison produced the highly popular sock-puppet program *Kukla, Fran and Ollie*. In 1949, Chicago radio host Dave Garroway premiered the television talk-show format, and several decades later, Chicagoan Oprah Winfrey became the nation's most successful and influential television personality.

Chicago retained its importance as an air transportation center, when in late 1945 the City Council accepted a World War II airfield—the 1,371-acre Orchard Place airport on the northwest side. Renamed in 1955 in honor of a World War II Navy hero, O'Hare International soon replaced Midway Airport in ranking among the world's busiest air terminals.

In 1940, Carl Sandburg had won the Pulitzer Prize in history for his six-volume biography of Abraham Lincoln. Then in 1950 Gwendolyn Brooks, author of poems and plays with African-American themes, became the first black woman to win the prize for her collection *Annie Allen*. In 1954, Oak Park native Ernest Hemingway was awarded the Nobel Prize in literature.

✧

Above: Chicago Sun newspapers with U.S. Victory headline are scattered in the street after a celebration in downtown Chicago hailing the end of WWII.
COURTESY OF THE CHICAGO HISTORICAL SOCIETY. PHOTOGRAPH; ICHI-37835.

Right: Illinois residents stepped forward to support the war effort by purchasing War Bonds. Shown here is Chicago's Howard Street Bond Booth.
COURTESY OF THE CHICAGO HISTORICAL SOCIETY. PHOTOGRAPHER - HENRY DELORVAL GREEN. PHOTOGRAPH; 1939-1945; ICHI-25620.

Architects in Illinois continued designing world-renowned structures. In Chicago, German-born Ludwig Mies Van Der Rohe planned a new campus for the Armour Institute (now the Illinois Institute of Technology). Coining the phrase "less is more," he designed stark yet elegant steel-and-glass buildings that included the Federal Center complex in Chicago and the airy Farnsworth House near Plano.

The postwar period brought increased suburban growth. Children began attending better-equipped and better-funded schools in consolidated districts in small-town and rural Illinois. By 1948 the number of school districts had been reduced by half, with the state shouldering a larger share of the financial burden. Southern Illinois State Normal School at Carbondale achieved university status, later expanding into the populous St. Clair-Madison counties area. The teachers' college at

Normal became Illinois State University, while the teacher-training schools at DeKalb, Macomb, and Charleston became state colleges, then universities.

In 1952 and again in 1956, the national Democratic party nominated as its presidential candidate Illinois Governor Adlai E. Stevenson, grandson of the former vice-president. As governor, he championed reform efforts in state government, along with education and welfare improvements. After losing both national elections to World War II hero Dwight D. Eisenhower, Stevenson was named by President John F. Kennedy as United States ambassador to the United Nations. "He imparted a nobility to public life," President Lyndon Johnson said on Stevenson's death in 1965, "and a grandeur to American purpose which has already reshaped the life of the nation and will endure for many generations."

✧

Adlai Stevenson, governor of Illinois from 1949-1953, ran for president in both 1952 and 1956, both times badly losing to Dwight Eisenhower. He later became the American ambassador to the United Nations during the John F. Kennedy administration. He is shown visiting the Stevenson for President headquarters in Chicago in 1956.

CHAPTER IX

CHANGING POPULATIONS, 1953-2000

Abraham Lincoln's state has advanced dramatically in the three hundred years since Jolliet and Marquette discovered the Illinois country and in the two centuries since George Rogers Clark made it part of the newly independent nation that became the United States. Illinois still has its central location, its rich soil and invigorating climate, and the other assets that have been utilized by a diverse, intelligent and resourceful people.

- Robert P. Howard, *Illinois: A History of the Prairie State*

With creation of the interstate highway system in the 1950s, Americans became an even more mobile society. Des Plaines salesman Ray A. Kroc revolutionized travelers' eating habits with McDonald's fast-food franchises he began in 1955. Thirty years later, McDonald's surpassed Sears, Roebuck & Co. as the nation's largest retail real-estate owner, and by 1995 the franchise empire swelled to fifteen thousand locations in some seventy countries.

The 1959 opening of the international St. Lawrence Seaway, linking the port of Chicago to the Atlantic Ocean, increased markets for midwestern agricultural and industrial products. In 1963, Democratic Governor Otto Kerner escorted businessmen on their first trade mission to Europe, and two years later he accompanied a group to Japan. By the following year, Illinois for the first time led the nation in exports of both agricultural and manufactured products, and by the end of the century became its leading soybean producer.

In 1958, the state's first nuclear power generating station was activated at the Dresden plant, along the Illinois River near Morris. By the end of the century, Illinois was home to the most nuclear plants in the nation—eleven reactors in six northern and central Illinois facilities, generating half of the state's energy needs. In 1966, Weston in DuPage County won "the scientific prize of the century," when the federal Atomic Energy Commission chose the small town, from more than two hundred potential sites, for the $250 million Fermi National Accelerator Laboratory. Fermilab houses the world's largest and most powerful atom accelerator for scientific research.

In order to make higher education opportunities available to all high school graduates, the General Assembly in 1965 passed the Public Junior College Act, creating independent junior college districts throughout the state. Now several hundred thousand students attend nearly fifty community colleges, administered by local boards and financed by local and state taxes and student tuition. In 1985, legislators established the innovative Illinois Mathematics and Science Academy in Aurora, a tax-supported residential high school with advanced courses in mathematics, science, arts, and humanities. The Academy also offers training programs for teachers throughout Illinois.

In southern Illinois during the 1960s, the Corps of Engineers created three lakes—Carlyle (the largest in the state), Rend, and Shelbyville—for flood control, community water supply, and recreation. Severe flooding of the state's rivers resulted on several occasions in major damage to farmland and towns. The most devastating flood in Illinois history occurred in 1993, when for four months nearly five thousand Army and Air National Guardsmen assisted local officials and residents struggling to maintain levees along a 400-mile span of Mississippi riverfront.

Immigration into the state continued, with the large numbers of Polish, Mexican, Italian, and German residents joined by new arrivals from eastern Europe and Asia. The mid-century economic boom also brought about a new period of innovation in architecture and community development, particularly in Chicago. In the late 1950s, architect Bertrand Goldberg's cylindrical-tower Marina

✧

Mayor Richard J. Daley is best remembered as the last "big boss" of Chicago. His long career as mayor began in 1955 and ended with his death in 1976.

COURTESY OF THE CHICAGO HISTORICAL SOCIETY. PHOTOGRAPH: ICHI-25726.

City along the Chicago River ranked among the most innovative structures. The 100-story John Hancock Building on Michigan Avenue became the world's tallest building until completion of the Sears Tower in 1974. Both were designed by Bruce Graham and Fazlur Kahn of the Skidmore, Owings, & Merrill (SOM) architectural firm. Architect Eero Saarinen designed headquarters buildings for the John Deere Company in Moline that complemented the prairie landscape, and in Wilmette stands the exquisite Baha'i Temple, designed by Louis Bourgeois.

In 1962, Lincoln biographer and Pulitzer Prize-recipient Carl Sandburg became the Poet Laureate of Illinois, followed by Gwendolyn Brooks in 1968. Saul Bellow won a Pulitzer Prize in 1975 for *Humboldt's Gift*, and a year later received the Nobel Prize in Literature. Louis "Studs" Terkel received a Pulitzer Prize in 1985 for *The Good War*, an oral history of the World War II years, and in 1989 *Chicago Tribune* columnist Clarence Page became the first African-American recipient of the award.

Earlier in the century, cities had begun provided public-financed housing for low-income residents. By the late 1950s, slum residences were being replaced with large complexes, many of which gradually hosted an array of social problems. In properties maintained by the Chicago Housing Authority, unemployment ran as high as ninety percent, and residents were at least twice as likely as other Chicagoans to be victims of serious crime. By the end of the century, a number of the housing projects were replaced with smaller buildings in less densely populated neighborhoods.

Politically, the Democratic party continued to dominate Chicago politics. Richard J. Daley, chairman of the Cook County Democratic committee and a consummate politician, won election as mayor in 1955. Reelected for five terms and serving for twenty-one years until his death in 1976, Daley garnered support from business leaders and a coalition of labor, ethnic groups, and blacks. He ran a powerful political machine, rewarding allies with patronage jobs, contracts, and well-maintained neighborhoods.

During the 1960s, Americans were again drawn into foreign conflict, this time in southeastern Asia. The United States supported South Vietnam, as communist-led guerrillas fought to overtake its government. Hostilities quickly escalated, with American

✧

Right: Although he left school at the young age of thirteen, Carl Sandburg went on to become a Pulitzer Prize-winning journalist and poet.

Below: Studs Terkel won the Pulitzer Prize in 1985 for The Good War, *an oral history of World War II. In addition to being a writer, Terkel was an accomplished musician and folklorist.*

troops eventually numbering more than five hundred thousand. Of those, nearly three thousand Illinoisans were reported killed or missing in action.

The war became a divisive political issue. During the 1968 Democratic National Convention, held in Chicago, massive anti-war protests and civil disorder led to 650 arrests and further destabilization of the already divided nation. While many in the media criticized the Chicago police for overreacting to the situation, Chicagoans generally approved of Daley's law-and-order approach. The chaos was cited as a major factor in the election later that year of Republican Richard M. Nixon. And for the next twenty-eight years, both parties shunned Chicago, which had hosted more political conventions by far than any other American city. Then in 1996, President Bill Clinton won his second-term Democratic nomination there.

After the 1968 assassination of civil rights leader Martin Luther King, Jr., race riots occurred in Washington, D.C., and many other places, including the Illinois cities of Chicago, Evanston, Maywood, East St. Louis, Alton, Aurora, Joliet, Chicago Heights, and Carbondale. Then in 1971 black Chicago political leader Jesse Jackson founded Operation PUSH—People United to Save

Humanity—becoming the most visible figure in the national civil rights movement. In 1979, Centralia native Roland W. Burris became comptroller, the first African American elected to statewide office in Illinois. After three terms, he won election in 1990 as the state's attorney general.

Another civil rights issue of the time was women's equality. In 1972, Congress passed the Equal Rights Amendment to provide equal treatment for males and females. The amendment required ratification by thirty-eight states to become part of the federal Constitution. But a leading opponent was conservative Republican Phyllis Schlafly of Alton; members of her "Stop ERA" movement convinced a majority of legislators to vote against the Illinois bill. By 1977, thirty-four states had ratified the amendment, but sixteen, including Illinois, had not—causing failure of the national effort.

In the late 1960s, lawmakers had begun considering replacing the hundred-year-old state constitution, and voters approved a convention to discuss relevant contemporary issues. Under Convention President Samuel W. Witwer, the members completed their task within a year, and voters ratified the new document in December 1970. Among the changes were liberalized amendment and constitutional convention processes. A home rule article allowed cities of at least twenty-five thousand population to levy taxes, issue certain licenses, borrow money, and pass ordinances without General Assembly approval. Also in 1970, the Illinois legislature was the first in the nation to adopt a comprehensive act safeguarding the state's environment, "consistent with the social and economic needs of the state."

With increasing demands for state services, in 1969 newly elected Republican Governor Richard B. Ogilvie had convinced legislators to enact a state income tax. Although the additional revenue was critical for maintaining programs, Democrat Dan Walker defeated Ogilvie four years later by reminding voters of his responsibility for the income tax.

The 1970 Constitution established that beginning in 1978, governors would be

✧

Chicago political activist Jesse Jackson has established himself as a leading spokesman for black political causes. An inspirational speaker, Jackson began his career as a foot soldier in the civil rights movement and has developed into a leader of millions of Americans, both black and white, who identify with Jackson's "rainbow coalition."
COURTESY OF THE LIBRARY OF CONGRESS.

✧

Above: Ronald Reagan, born in Tampico, Illinois, was the forty-first president of the United States, serving from 1981 to 1989. After a successful acting career he entered politics in California and was elected to two terms as governor.

COURTESY OF THE SANGAMON VALLEY COLLECTION AT LINCOLN LIBRARY, SPRINGFIELD

Right: Few people believed that Jane Byrne held any chance of defeating Michael Bilandic in Chicago's 1978 mayoral election until Chicago was virtually paralyzed by a series of severe snowstorms that caused many to lose faith in Bilandic's ability to keep the city working, giving Byrne the edge needed to win and her place in history as the first female mayor of Chicago.

COURTESY OF THE CHICAGO HISTORICAL SOCIETY.

elected in non-presidential election years. The 1976 candidates for a two-year term were Democratic Secretary of State Michael Howlett and Republican Chicago attorney James R. Thompson. By attracting independent as well as Democratic voters, Thompson won the first of four consecutive terms as the state's chief executive. In the 1982 election, he defeated former Senator Adlai E. Stevenson III by little more than five thousand votes—the closest statewide election in modern history.

In 1980, Illinois native Ronald Reagan was elected President of the United States, defeating the Democratic incumbent Jimmy Carter as well as Rockford Independent candidate John B. Anderson. Born in Tampico and reared in Dixon, Reagan, the former motion-picture actor and California governor, won reelection in 1984 during a period of economic prosperity. Although Reagan's Illinois victory was a statewide Republican landslide, Democrat Paul Simon, a former state legislator, lieutenant governor, and congressman, won election to the U.S. Senate.

In Chicago in 1979, Daley's consumer affairs commissioner, Jane Byrne, had garnered more than eighty percent of the vote in winning election as the city's first female mayor. But four years later, with a shrinking tax base and limited opportunities for

minorities, she faced Democratic primary opposition from Congressman Harold Washington and Cook County State's Attorney Richard M. Daley, son of the former mayor. A black activist from the city's south side, Washington won with thirty-six percent of the vote, then defeated Republican state legislator Bernard Epton in the general election. Washington received 97 percent of the black vote and more than 50 percent of the Hispanic vote. He easily won reelection in 1987 and gained control of the City Council, but within the year died of a heart attack at his City Hall desk. Then in 1989, Daley was elected to the first of five terms as Chicago mayor.

Just as the Illinois economy changed from agricultural to industrial in the late nineteenth century, a national recession in the 1970s led to a serious and continuing decline in the state's industrial base. Scores of plants closed throughout Illinois, particularly in the Chicago, Rockford, Peoria, and East St. Louis areas, with thousands of lost jobs in steel, coal, farm implements, and other heavy manufacturing industries. Over succeeding years, technology and service economies gradually replaced much of the industrial economy.

Those losses created tremendous challenges for workers and their unions. Whereas in the 1950s, one-third of private sector workers held union membership (which brought higher wages, better benefits, pensions, and increased job security), by the end of the century, the rate had fallen to less than ten percent. At the same time, public sector unions increased, including the Illinois Education Association and the Association of Federal, State, County, and Municipal Employees.

In Decatur in 1993, after resisting management work-rules and hours changes, workers at A. E. Staley (newly purchased by British conglomerate Tate & Lyle) were locked out of the soybean-processing plant. The situation lasted for two years, until a slim majority of the employees accepted a contract offer they had overwhelmingly rejected in 1992. In 1994, union members at Caterpillar plants in central Illinois began a series of strikes that continued until 1998, while the Decatur Bridgestone/Firestone plant closed following strikes over issues that included the imposition of twelve-hour shifts.

In 1984, although Chicago was eclipsed by Los Angeles as second in population to New York, the "collar county" communities surrounding Cook County experienced enormous growth. By then, Illinois had long since evolved politically into three regions: Democratic Chicago and surrounding Cook County, Republican collar counties, and a combination in the rest of the state. Sangamon County, the seat of Illinois government, has remained traditionally Republican.

In sports, the Chicago Bulls in 1991 won the first of three consecutive National Basketball Association championships, then repeated the achievement between 1996 and 1998. Team member Michael Jordan set an NBA record with eight scoring titles and four Most Valuable Player designations. In 1994, Champaign speed skater Bonnie Blair won five Olympic gold medals, the most by an American female competitor.

Illinois, which in 1818 had been the least-populated state ever admitted to the union, entered the twenty-first century as the nation's most populous inland state and sixth in number of inhabitants.

✧

Left: Michael Jordan led the Chicago Bulls to five NBA championships in the 1990s. Jordan has been described by many as "the best player to ever play the game."

Below: Barak Obama was elected United States senator in 2004. Prior to his election, Obama served seven years in the Illinois state senate.

COURTESY OF OBAMA FOR ILLINOIS, INC.

CHAPTER X

ILLINOIS IN THE TWENTY-FIRST CENTURY

Illinois, that long slice of the heartland stretching from Lake Michigan to Kentucky, may be the most American place of all. Its great patriot, Abraham Lincoln, and its great athlete, Michael Jordan, stand for what's best about our country....

Illinois remains both urban and rural at once. And flatness, it turns out, is good for much: operating farm equipment, riding bikes, walking far, erecting tall buildings, seeing a long way off. People stand out in a flat landscape, as does what they build. Native Americans, before they were driven from Illinois, constructed thousands of ceremonial and burial mounds, now so much a part of the landscape as to be one with it. These days Illinois builds skyscrapers instead, but the principle is the same. They are leaving their mark.

- Joanne Trestrail, *Illinois: The Spirit of America*

Today's Land of Lincoln, also known as the Inland Empire and the Prairie State, comprises nearly 12.5 million residents, an 8.6 percent growth from the 1990 federal census. Median family income in Illinois increased nearly 11 percent during the 1990s, with a significant decrease in the number of poverty-level households. "Economic conditions for the average Illinois family improved significantly over the last decade," reported Governor George H. Ryan in 2001. "We're seeing more Illinoisans graduating from high school and pursuing post-secondary instruction levels, which bodes well for a continued increase in the quality of life for our residents."

Entering the new century, Chicago retained its status as the dominant city in Illinois. Rockford, the state's second largest city, continues as the hub of an extensive northern agricultural region. The Chicago-area communities of Aurora and Naperville are now the third and fourth largest cities, with population increases of nearly fifty percent during the past decade. The state's diversity is reflected in the number of foreign-born residents, which grew more than sixty percent in the 1990s. In Chicago, most of the European ethnic enclaves have been replaced by other immigrant and racial groups, especially those of Mexican, Puerto Rican, and Chinese heritage.

Illinois soil ranks among the most fertile in the nation, with thousands of farms covering nearly eighty percent of the total land area. Soybeans, corn, cattle, and hogs are the primary products, along with wheat, oats, alfalfa, hay, sorghum, fruits, and vegetables. Still, farmland is being converted to suburban industrial and residential use at the rate of one hundred thousand acres annually. "We spend a lot of money to attract new industry to the state," warned an Illinois Department of Agriculture specialist, "but the biggest industry is agriculture, and we need to keep it that way."

Food processing is the state's primary manufacturing activity. Illinois ranks second nationally in the export of agricultural commodities, primarily soybeans, feed grains, and related products. Illinois corn provides the nation's largest supply of ethanol fuel, and in Decatur are headquartered the grain conglomerate Archer Daniels Midland and soybean processor A. E. Staley. Deere & Company in Moline, which began in 1837 with John Deere's invention of a self-scouring steel plow, is the world's leading manufacturer of farm implements.

In addition to agricultural products and equipment, major elements of the current economy are in the fields of education, healthcare, finance, insurance, computer technology, telecommunications, utilities, transportation, corrections, riverboat gambling, and tourism.

Illinois is sixth among the states in coal production, with more than forty million tons mined each year. The largest markets for Illinois' high-energy bituminous coal are midwestern and southern electric utility companies and European countries.

✧

The Eads Bridge, built by James Buchanan Eads and completed in 1874, is on the National Register of Historic Places. The bridge is the first across the Mississippi River below the Missouri River, the first to rely heavily on steel, and the first to use cantilever construction. Today the Eads Bridge is open to vehicle traffic during the week and open to pedestrians and bicycles on weekends.

Oil extraction is not as profitable today as in mid-century, because plentiful overseas supplies lowered crude oil prices to levels at which many of the state's independent producers could no longer compete. From a peak annual production of nearly eighty million barrels, the current yield is 10 to 12 million barrels from forty of the state's 102 counties.

To facilitate product marketing and distribution, Illinois maintains an extensive system of roads and bridges. Rail networks are located along the Mississippi in Madison and St. Clair counties and in Chicago, which is also the principal North American hub for freight trucking. Among the many public-access airports in Illinois, O'Hare International in Chicago is the largest and busiest, although studies indicate a continuing need for increased capacity. World headquarters for both United Airlines and the aircraft manufacturer Boeing are located in Chicago. The city and its suburbs are also home to numerous international firms, including McDonald's, Motorola, Sara Lee, Sears, and Walgreens.

Modern waterways connect the state with industrial centers from Canada to the Gulf of Mexico. Nearly half of all commercial Mississippi traffic above St. Louis comes through the Illinois River. The state's rivers, tributaries, and lakes also provide urban and rural water supplies, along with recreational fishing, boating, and waterfowl hunting.

✧

Donald Rumsfeld served as Secretary of State under President George W. Bush and previously as Secretary of State and Chief of Staff under President Gerald Ford. He also served in the Richard Nixon administration. Rumsfeld was elected to the U.S. Congress from the Chicago suburbs in 1962 at the age of thirty, and was re-elected to three additional terms.

COURTESY OF THE U.S. DEPARTMENT OF DEFENSE.

Below: The State Capitol in Springfield as it appears today.

COURTESY OF THE SPRINGFIELD CONVENTION & VISITORS BUREAU.

The Illinois economy in the new century began slipping from record growth of the 1990s, as the number of residents working in agriculture and related industries fell by nearly fifty percent. Employment in manufacturing and technology fields also declined, with the result that state and local governments have begun providing economic incentives to domestic and foreign companies in order to stimulate business development.

In 2001, Governor Ryan commissioned an in-depth study of the state's capital punishment laws and procedures. In January 2003—at the close of his gubernatorial term—he cited the report's finding of a "flawed" death-penalty process in issuing a blanket commutation for the more than 160 death-row inmates. That decision spurred a continuing national controversy between pro- and anti-death penalty advocates.

The election of Ryan's successor, Rod Blagojevich, and other state officials brought the return of Democratic officeholders following a quarter-century of Republican control. Upon assuming office, however, Governor Blagojevich and the Democratic-controlled General Assembly faced a more than $4-billion budget deficit, resulting from both national and state economic declines.

In the aftermath of the horrific September 2001 terrorist attacks in New York and

Washington, D.C., former Illinois congressman and current Secretary of Defense Donald Rumsfeld helped lead the nation's retaliation against enemy forces in the south-central Asian nation of Afghanistan. "The United States of America," he said at the time, "represents something so important to the world—our free way of life. If you care about human beings, you have to care that the U.S. model, which benefits not just the people in our country but across the globe, succeeds."

The Illinois National Guard is helping to provide both state and national security. From fifty-three armories, members of the Army and Air National Guard train for emergency assignment in Illinois and throughout the world. Recent deployments have included terrorist regions of the Persian Gulf.

Illinoisans look to the future with new opportunities to reflect on many aspects of the state's significant past. The Chicago Historical Society offers programs and exhibits to expand interest in area history, while supporting a large library and publications program. In Springfield, an important recent resource is the Abraham Lincoln Presidential Library and Museum. This center for the study of Lincoln and the American Civil War houses the State Historical Library and its premier collection of Lincoln papers and artifacts, along with innumerable materials on other facets of Illinois history.

Archaeology is another resource for continuing historical research. In Pike County, historians and anthropologists from the University of Illinois/Springfield have begun preserving and recreating the African-American frontier settlement of New Philadelphia. In the deep southern portion of the state, between the Ohio and Mississippi rivers, Southern Illinois University/Carbondale faculty and students search for evidence of Late Woodland (A.D. 600-900) villages, French settlements, and an 1800 army fort, along with Civil War shipyards, structures, and contraband camps at Cairo.

The National Register of Historic Places lists nearly sixteen hundred sites within the state. In addition, the Illinois Historic Preservation Agency manages more than fifty state-owned places and hosts a variety of special events. In Madison County, a new IHPA visitor center commemorates Camp Dubois, the 1803-1804 winter encampment of Meriwether Lewis and William Clark, from which they launched their epic Corps of Discovery expedition to the Pacific Northwest.

Throughout Illinois, innumerable members of county and local historical, genealogical, and museum organizations are guardians and caretakers of historic buildings and research collections. Together, these historians, students, genealogists, and other interested individuals strive to preserve the myriad elements of our state's incomparable heritage.

✧

The modern Chicago skyline provides an impressive backdrop to boats anchored in the harbor.

COURTESY OF THE CHICAGO CONVENTION AND TOURISM BUREAU.

✧

Jolliet and Marquette, August 1673 *by*
Robert Thom. The painting was
commissioned for the Illinois State
Sesquicentennial celebration.

COURTESY OF THE ILLINOIS STATE HISTORICAL SOCIETY.

SHARING THE HERITAGE

historic profiles of businesses,

organizations, and families that

have contributed to the development

and economic base of Illinois

SPECIAL THANKS TO

*Chicago Automobile
Trade Association*

Connor Company

*Illinois Education
Association*

Kroeschell, Inc.

RENAISSANCE SPRINGFIELD HOTEL

Renaissance is a fitting name for the landmark hotel in downtown Springfield that is a symbol of the rebirth of the city's central area. The Renaissance harkens back to the days of grand hotels with luxurious appointments and impeccable service. At its opening the prestigious *Chicago Architectural Annual* noted the new Renaissance was "a handsomely detailed and Neoclassically inspired 316-room hotel (it) relates to Illinois' capital by breaking up its large mass and by attempting a recall of existing turn-of-the-century buildings with its articulated red brick and limestone cladding."

While affiliated with a national hotel group, the Renaissance was, in many ways, the creation of Springfield developer Bill Cellini and his wife, Julie. From the initial dream of adding a first class hotel to the city skyline, through design, construction and furnishing, the Cellinis were intimately involved with every detail. The result is a personality and style far beyond that found in a typical hotel. This is evident from the first step into the marble floored lobby with its authentic nineteenth century antique furnishings, personally selected by Julie Cellini. The twenty-two custom-made crystal chandeliers invitingly arranged throughout the first floor come from the Island of Murano, near Venice and were acquired by the Cellinis during an Italian vacation. Brass hardware and gold leaf mirror frames contrast with rich, dark woods in the lobby. Audubon prints and cherry wood furnishings lend dignity and elegance to guest rooms.

But lavish furnishings and luxury construction are only a part of the Renaissance story. "From the first class accommodations to gracious personal service, the 316-room hotel has a reputation for excellence among business and vacation travelers." Renaissance guests are treated to cable television, movies and video games, courtesy in-room coffee, tea, irons, ironing boards, hair dryers and toiletries. Services and amenities are first quality.

Conventions are a big business in the capital city and the Renaissance is readily equipped to handle every kind of function from symposiums to business meetings to social gatherings. Located on the lobby level the Renaissance Ballroom, with over 6,000 square feet, can hold up to 700 people. This well planned room has an antechamber where registration can take place and vendors can set up displays. The ballroom itself can be divided into four "salons" so that separate meetings may be held at the same time. On the second level of the hotel are four hospitality suites named after famous Illinois governors—Altgeld, Bond, Horner, and Yates, the Freeport and Ottawa Rooms and various small boardrooms. Both the Freeport and Ottawa Rooms can be partitioned off or opened depending on the size of the function.

Catering menus ranging from coffee breaks to full course dinners are offered for these events. Breakfast, luncheon and dinner selections have a number of reasonably priced meals to choose from. A wide range of cocktails, beer and wine are available as well.

Conveniently located immediately east of the Renaissance is the Prairie Capital Convention Center, which hosts a variety of functions including trade shows, sporting events and concerts. The center's main floor offers forty-four thousand square feet of exhibiting space with versatile setup arrangements of partitions. A custom lighting

and sound system is available for use of exhibitors. The Center was designed for nearly any type of event including "basketball, wrestling, circuses, ice shows, trade shows, lectures, theatre, symphony concerts, opera, ballet and conventions." An adjacent six-level parking garage accommodates 750 cars. An underground tunnel connects the Renaissance with this versatile facility.

The top two floors of the Renaissance are private-key access area, offering larger rooms, free standing, full-length mirrors, marble topped coffee tables and the feel of a luxurious private home. Guests there have access to the Club Lounge with its beautiful view of the city, where a continental breakfast and evening hors d'oeuvres and discounted cordials are served. Also on the top floors are the Presidential and Governor's Suites, which presidents have used and where governors have slept. The suites have living rooms and dining rooms furnished with high style antiques and include kitchens, wet bars, sunken tubs, and king-size four-poster beds.

The Concourse Level houses the hotel's large swimming pool, for a relaxing swim after a long day. Some guests prefer to unwind with a workout in the health club where a full range of physical fitness equipment is available and then enjoy the soothing effects of the whirlpool or the redwood sauna.

Diners have a choice of several options for their eating pleasure. Within the hotel are two excellent eating establishments. Lindsay's Gallery Restaurant, named after famed Springfield poet Vachel Lindsay, serves breakfast, lunch and dinner. This popular eatery, which features reproductions of Lindsay's artwork, is renowned for its luncheon buffets and spectacular Sunday Brunch. Named after the inn where Abraham Lincoln and his young bride, Mary, first took up housekeeping, the Globe Tavern also serves light lunches and snacks during the day in a casual pub atmosphere. Crowds gather there at night to enjoy a cocktail and to relax. A variety of fine restaurants are scattered throughout the downtown area offering a varied cuisine for both lunch and dinner as well.

Located in the heart of Springfield's downtown, the Renaissance is close by many Abraham Lincoln and other tourist

sites. The Lincoln Home National Historic Site sits just three blocks south of the hotel. Centered in a historic four-block area, the home is open yearround and tours are free to the public. Lincoln gave his farewell address to Springfield residents at the historic Great Western Depot situated on the railroad tracks just two blocks east of the Renaissance hotel.

Other sites related to Lincoln's career as a lawyer and politician is located on the city's historic downtown public square. The Lincoln-Herndon Law Office has been restored to the time period when Lincoln occupied it. The Greek-Revival Illinois Old State Capitol was completely torn down and rebuilt to accurately portray Illinois state government two centuries ago. It has been called the most historic building west of the Alleghenies. Both the law office and Capitol are maintained by the State of Illinois and are open to the public. The Abraham Lincoln Presidential Library and Museum, just north of the square, promises to become a prominent place for Lincoln scholars to do research, as the rest of the public is educated about the life of this great man. The library portion opened in the spring of 2003 while the museum opened in April 2005. Springfield's historic Oak Ridge Cemetery, on the city's far north side, is the home to the Lincoln Monument, which serves as the president's final resting place.

But the downtown generally offers much for the visitor. There is shopping in specialty stores—clothing, cards, gifts, florists and even a vintage record store—all within a short walking distance of the Renaissance. There are dozens of restaurants and a lively nightlife. A new arts center offers a changing venue. Politics in the flesh, one of Springfield's most popular forms of entertainment, is only a few blocks from the Renaissance door. The State Capitol Complex forms the western boundary of Springfield's downtown.

Shuttle service to and from the Amtrak Station or Capital Airport is provided. Valet or self-service parking in the adjacent parking garage eases arrivals and departures whether for the business traveler midweek or families enjoying the weekend. A warm

welcome and courteous service is a hallmark of Renaissance life. And, this service makes each visit special. The key to this service is an outstanding experienced professional staff of two hundred-plus. From the waiter in the Globe Tavern or the attendant that takes care of each and every guest room, it is the staff that makes every stay at the Renaissance a memorable experience.

MARSHALL FIELD'S

Innovative and exciting, enduring and classic as Chicago itself, Marshall Field's is a name that conjures elegance, high style and always the unexpected. For more than 150 years, shopping in Chicago has been defined by a singular experience—Marshall Field's. From the very beginning it was clear Field's would be no ordinary place but rather a world apart from the general merchandise stores then common. Over the years, Field's has become recognized internationally as a leader in retailing with a stunning number of "firsts" to its credit. A few of these pioneering trends include the first bridal registry program in the United States, the first private label merchandise and establishment of a liberal return policy based on the phrase coined by Marshall Field that "the customer is always right." Revolving credit was another boon to shoppers in the early days. Although rich in tradition, the essence of Field's experience today is an array of merchandise, services and stores that are both innovative and timeless.

Innovation and trend setting has been a way of life since the founding of the business by Chicago luminary Potter Palmer in 1852. Palmer's first store at 137 Lake Street carried the same dry goods as dozens of his competitors but it was his sales strategy that

set the establishment apart. Women, who had been largely ignored by merchants, became the target customers. A liberal policy allowed the return of any item for any reason. This innovative strategy made the store phenomenally successful and Palmer took in a junior partner, Marshall Field, who brought along businessman and colleague Levi Leiter. Field and Leiter emphasized a stock of first quality, fashionable and luxurious goods, which dazzled customers who formed a loyal and growing base. Palmer, Field and Leiter reaped fabulous personal fortunes from their genius. Palmer used his new wealth to become a real estate mogul but Field & Leiter used theirs to purchase the company in 1867.

The following year, the store moved to a grand, newly completed, white marble building, commonly called the "Marble Palace," where luxurious goods lined the aisles along with well-dressed sales people ready to serve. Nineteenth century grand department stores were not only places of commerce but also centers of entertainment and education. Customers could discover the latest fashions but also see ensembles of clothing and settings for household goods. And Field's was fast-becoming the grandest of these emporiums where all customers—not just wealthy—were welcomed and treated with great courtesy. In 1871, Field's established the first foreign buying office of any American retailer, filling his store with European and other imports, then considered some of the world's most

❖

Above: Marshall Field, c. 1885.

Below: The main aisle, first floor, Marshall Field's State Street store. Holiday displays designed by Arthur Fraser, December 1934.

fashionable goods. But Field cannily mixed in moderately priced items with those of great cost. At the height of this success, the Great Chicago Fire leveled his store and much of the city. Marshall Field's loss was estimated at $2.5 million, equivalent to nearly $35 million today. But Field took no time to regret his misfortune. Rather he sprang into action, paying all staff on time, inspiring great loyalty with this staff and earning the respect of the greater community. Two weeks after the fire, Field and his staff opened an outlet in a surviving horse barn with fresh-ordered stock. In less than two years Field and Leiter opened in a rebuilt store. In a devastating repeat of history that new building burned to the ground in 1877.

The indomitable Field replaced that lost structure with a more impressive one and patrons flocked to its reopening in 1879, which proved to be the beginning of even palmier days for Chicago's newly crowned "Merchant Prince." After Leiter's retirement in 1881, Marshall Field & Company found two new executives, John Shedd and Harry Selfridge, who engineered continued achievements into the twentieth century. Selfridge went on to found the famous London department store Selfridge's. When Field died in 1906, he was among the wealthiest men in the world and his name lives on in the store and world-renowned Field Museum for which he left $8 million in his will.

The 1890s were times of great creative innovations for the store that had become a Chicago institution under Shedd and Selfridge's guidance. A tearoom that opened in 1890 became the ancestor of the famed Walnut Room where guests continue to dine today. Immense plate glass display windows were installed around the perimeter of the store, featuring

professionally designed dramatic displays by Arthur Fraser that drew admiring crowds. A genuine piece of Americana was born with the installation of the large clock at the corner of State and Washington Streets in 1897 and a second one at State and Randolph a few years later. Norman Rockwell would immortalize the clock in 1945 when he depicted the clock at State and Randolph having its hands being set to the pocket watch of a clock mender. But the most enduring Field's accomplishment of that time was the demolition of the 1879 structure and construction of the present building, which began in 1892. Like a great temple or cathedral, the building took many years to complete, being finished in 1914.

Daniel Burnham, internationally known Chicago architect and main designer of the famed Chicago Columbian Exposition of 1893, designed the new building which was, and still is, best described in superlatives. More than 2 million square feet of floor space is covered with 31 miles of carpeting, serviced by 24 elevators, 40 escalators and 23,000 fire sprinklers. The nine-story, 165-foot-atrium and heroically proportioned 50-foot granite columns at the State Street entrance (reputed to be the tallest on the continent) continually impress visitors. But the most breathtaking architectural feature without a doubt is the 6,000-square-foot vaulted ceiling fitted with 1.6 million pieces of Tiffany glass in a Renaissance Revival-Style architectural framework. Its Byzantine splendor has awed customers since 1907.

Field's not only reflected the latest in fashion but began to influence it as well. Women's styles were featured in a store magazine, *Fashions of the Hour*, which began publication in 1914. Men were courted with the opening of a new gentleman's clothing department that same year. But it was the opening of The 28 Shop in 1941 that gave Field's a true fashion presence in the United States. This shop-within-a-shop was reminiscent of Parisian fashion salons and its lavish, theatrical interior was a Chicago centerpiece for eagerly awaited new styles.

From introduction of escalators in 1934 to animated store windows, technological innovations have served Field's public and kept them entertained through the years. And

✧

Above: The corner of State and Washington Streets, featuring Marshall Field's Great Clock, October 1927.

Below: The Louis Comfort Tiffany Ceiling, the world's largest unbroken Tiffany vaulted ceiling, installed in 1907, c. 2001.
COURTESY OF HEDRICH-BLESSING.

✧

Above: The beauty department on the main aisle on the first floor of Marshall Field's State Street store, October 2002.

Below: The Vertical Fashion Show on the façade of the store along State Street, September 2003.

holidays, especially Christmas, are marked with special festivity in the store. The Great Tree, which has graced the Walnut Room since 1907, is watched over by Marshall Field's very own Uncle Mistletoe and eating a meal and viewing the tree has become a quintessential family tradition, charming hundreds of thousands of visitors annually.

Public service has been deeply ingrained in Field's leadership. Beginning with Marshall Field's donation of clothes and blankets to residents after the 1871 fire, Field's executives and team members have been at the forefront of civic involvement, from bond drives to charity fundraising. In 1946, Marshall Field's

became a member of the "Five Percent Club," a landmark movement that encourages U.S. corporations to commit five percent of federally taxable income to support nonprofits. Marshall Fields' Gives, the company's umbrella giving program, supports commendable causes that inspire children to read and learn, arts and cultural organizations and social service programs.

An ability to change while maintaining the best of its traditions has kept Marshall Field's successful and viable amidst the changing economic climate over the decades. In the 1930s the fiscally conservative store smoothly weathered the Great Depression. During the years of postwar expansion in the 1940s and 1950s, Field's leadership anticipated the growing importance of suburban marketing and opened its Old Orchard shopping center in Skokie, Illinois, featuring a 310,000-square-foot store. More than a dozen Marshall Field's stores followed in the next decades.

In 2003, Marshall Field's reinforced its status as the premier retail and entertainment destination by transforming more than 800,000 square feet of retail space at its flagship State Street store. This "Renaissance of Retail" continues Field's tradition of delivering the expected and unexpected by adding hundreds of new vendors and exclusive merchandise across its stores, injecting newness and cutting-edge fashion into merchandising assortments and enhancing Field's already famous reputation for guest service.

For more than 130 years Marshall Field's has represented the finest in shopping experiences. The stunningly restored architectural gem of its flagship store successfully marries tradition to newness in every field—clothing, furnishings, accessories, cosmetics and surprising partnerships with famous merchandisers from around the world. But it doesn't end there. A recent vertical fashion show, another first for Marshall Field's, sent a thunderbolt through the fashion industry worldwide.

Like its hometown of Chicago, Marshall Field's constantly reinvents itself—while maintaining its revered traditions and, always, the highest-quality offerings and guest service. The Field's experience has become, in the words of the *Chicago Tribune*, "As Chicago as it Gets."

HITZEMAN FUNERAL HOME LTD.

Community service and tradition are two hallmarks of Hitzeman Funeral Home Ltd. of Brookfield, Illinois. German-born Frederick H. Hitzeman gave up the tailor trade in 1904 to start an undertaking business at 4115 West Twenty-sixth Street in Chicago, Illinois. The first funeral parlor was opened in the Hitzeman home utilizing the first floor for business with the second floor as living quarters. Charles R. Hitzeman, the third of fifteen children born to Frederick and Pauline Hitzeman, started working with his father in 1915 as a carriage driver for funerals. After the change to automobiles, Charles drove the hearse. Due to a growing need and to provide better service, Frederick built a new two-story brick funeral home in 1922. Charles became a full partner with his father in 1928.

Norbert F. Hitzeman, Charles' son, entered the funeral business in 1951 as his father's partner and spent the first five years of his career as an embalmer. In 1955 plans began under Norbert's direction to build a new funeral home in Brookfield on land obtained by Frederick from a defaulted loan. After several attempts to obtain a required variance in zoning laws, the funeral home was completed in 1962 and opened for business in 1963. The Chicago funeral home was sold in 1976. The following year, Charles retired from active participation in the business with Norbert taking over and purchasing it outright in 1984. The fourth generation of the family, Todd N. Hitzeman, graduated in 1975 from the same mortuary school as his father and grandfather. He joined the firm soon after and purchased it upon the retirement of his father in 1995. Jan Hitzeman,

Todd's sister, received her degree and was, for a time, associated with the family business. Todd's son, Charles T. "Chuck" Hitzeman, became the fifth and latest generation of the family in the business when in 2003, he became a licensed funeral director and embalmer.

Community involvement has been an important priority followed by each generation of the Hitzeman family. Family members have been active in organizations including the Lions International, Brookfield Chamber of Commerce, school and religious organizations. This extensive community service allows the Hitzemans to better understand the needs of the generations of families they continue to serve.

Five generations of Hitzemans have served in this family-owned and operated business since 1904. Its centennial anniversary was celebrated in 2004. The Hitzemans look forward to continued dignified and high-quality service for another century.

✧

Above Five generations at the present location in Brookfield (from left to right): Charles T. Hitzeman (fifth generation), Todd N. Hitzeman (fourth generation), Frederick H. Hitzeman (first generation), Charles R. Hitzeman (second generation), and Norbert F. Hitzeman (third generation).

Below: The beginnings of a century-old business located at Twenty-sixth and Keeler in Chicago, Illinois.

ROBERT MORRIS COLLEGE

Robert Morris College is an institution that never stands still. Always with an eye on the future, RMC consistently plans for the world that will be, not just the world of today. As a private, not-for-profit, accredited college, it grants bachelor and associate degrees and has an enrollment of over 6,300 students.

Curricula are developed with input from leaders in business, technology, culinary and health fields. The programs are focused on the most in-demand jobs in the fastest growing industries. The goal is not only to educate students, but also to prepare them for careers that make them valuable contributors to society.

RMC also goes the extra mile to make a quality education convenient, accessible and affordable for any student with the desire for self-improvement.

Robert Morris College was originally chartered as a junior college in Carthage, Illinois in 1965. Named for a financier and patriot of the American Revolution, the school's roots go back nearly a century—to 1913. That year, Chicago's Moser School was founded and later merged with Robert Morris College.

RMC began an aggressive expansion program throughout Illinois with the move of the Carthage campus to Springfield in 1988. As a result, RMC set its main campus in Chicago and over the years established six branch campuses in Lake County, DuPage, Bensonville, Orland Park, Peoria and Springfield.

Courses of study are offered through the School of Business Administration, the Institute of Culinary Arts, the School of Health Studies, the Institute of Art and Design and the School of Computer Studies. RMC programs are unique. Students begin coursework in their fields of study during their first quarter on campus. This lets them become familiar sooner with their planned career field. Support comes from dedicated, caring and qualified faculty members. A student may complete a bachelor's degree in less than four years or an associate degree in as little as fifteen months.

The College offers the distinctive combination of accelerated programs, focused instruction and one of the lowest tuition rates in the state. And although it is one of the largest private colleges around, class sizes are some of the smallest and graduation rates are among the highest. Other national distinctions include: the top provider of bachelor's degrees in business by a private college in Illinois, one of the top providers of bachelor's degrees in business to minorities, the nation's top provider of associate degrees in business management, and a national top fifteen provider of bachelor degrees in computer studies to Hispanics.

The College's mission is to provide students from diverse backgrounds with the foundation needed to meet the expectations of business and society. To achieve its goals, RMC is dedicated to:

- Growth: To provide the opportunity for an RMC education to an increasing number of students.
- Improvement: To continually improve program offerings and the delivery of services.
- Viability: To manage scarce resources with efficiency.
- Enrichment: To attract and keep faculty and staff who are committed to exemplary performance, the mission of the College and personal and professional development.

Robert Morris College takes great pride in the quality, caliber, dedication and professionalism of its faculty. The College actively seeks out individuals who not only hold advanced degrees and are knowledgeable in their fields of study, but who are able to bring successful experience to their students and their respective departments.

✧

From left to right; Robert Morris, General George Washington, and Haym Salomon. Morris and Salomon were financiers of the Revolutionary War.

As a leader in applied education, Robert Morris College encourages faculty members to be involved in their subjects through continued study, outside consulting, writing for specialized publications, community service and memberships in professional organizations.

Instructors are available to students for tutoring, program direction, mentoring and guidance. They are dedicated to the continued achievements of their students. When a Robert Morris College student reaches his or her goal, the entire College succeeds.

Advisors also help students with housing, interviewing skills and networking techniques. Students maintain close, regular contacts with their program advisors to discuss problems and plans for achieving educational goals. A special office of Career Services helps students map successful career courses. RMC graduates also take advantage of the Alumni Office events that provide networking opportunities and inside track, personal contacts.

RMC's high quality of education and its affordability offer an appeal to a wide range of students. Financial assistance plans range from merit-based scholarships and need based financial aid, to athletic scholarships and tailored payment plans. Admissions and funding representatives assist in completing

applications for financial aid and help match students to available grants and loans.

RMC scholarships include the Academic Distinction Scholarship for full tuition, the Academic Achievement Scholarship with up to $15,000 awarded toward a bachelor's degree, as well as the Ben Franklin Scholarship for incoming freshmen. Specialized art, interior design, fitness specialist, culinary, computer studies and athletic scholarships complement RMC's financial aid component.

There is a program or combination of programs tailored for every student and prospective student. Additional information on financial assistance is available on the College's website, www.robertmorris.edu. Financial aid counselors and scholarship

✧

Above: Robert Morris College provides life-long placement assistance for its graduates.

Below: Robert Morris College's main campus is on the corner of State and Congress in the landmark Second Leiter Building.

advisors are also available to meet with students for further information.

The successful combination of highest-quality education, strong support for students and focused learning ensures a high success rate for RMC graduates. The placement rate for bachelor's degree graduates is over ninety-six percent. Much of this success comes from the attitudes and work ethic cultivated in a daily atmosphere. Over seventy percent of students participate in extracurricular activities. Internships are incorporated throughout the curriculum. Community involvement is encouraged for every student as well.

The network of seven RMC campuses extends from Lake County in the northern tip of Illinois to Springfield in the center of the State. In Chicago, RMC is housed in an historic landmark building across from the Harold Washington Library and in proximity to the Art Institute, Field Museum, Museum of Contemporary Art, Board of Trade, Merchandise Mart, theater district and the vibrant central district of this famed American city. Other Chicago-area locations include Aurora, Orland Park and Bensonville near O'Hare, as well as Lake County in Waukegan. The Peoria campus is located in the heart of the business district. The state capital campus in Springfield serves central and southern Illinois. Robert Morris is fully accredited by the Higher Learning Commission of the North Central Association.

In addition to the academic offerings Robert Morris College has a vibrant athletic program as well. There are opportunities to participate in men's and women's basketball, cross-country, golf, hockey and soccer along with men's baseball and women's softball, tennis, track, bowling and volleyball. And at Robert Morris, success in sports is just as apparent as in academics. Once again, the Lady Eagles Hockey team recently finished their regular season as national champs, ranked number one in the nation.

The future is indeed bright for Robert Morris College and its graduates. RMC strives to provide a well-rounded education and personal development with art shows and poetry readings and other extracurricular offerings as part of student life. Robert Morris has become one of the largest private colleges in the state of Illinois by providing a first-rate, quality education at an accelerated pace. The College constantly adapts to meet market changes and its curriculum supports areas of strong employer demand. This educational experience is offered at an affordable price with over seventy percent of all Robert Morris students receiving some form of financial assistance. All of this makes a Robert Morris education an invaluable personal and pro-fessional experience, an experience developed through excellence, passion and innovation—a place where dreams find direction.

✧

Robert Morris College works with leaders in the business, technology, culinary, and healthcare fields to provide current and relevant courses for its students.

PASSAVANT AREA HOSPITAL

Passavant Area Hospital was visualized as an orphanage in the eye of its original benefactor. But Morgan County took care of orphans through relatives and friends, and although the city of Jacksonville had fourteen physicians, one homeopath, one chiropodist, and six dentists—it had no hospital. Eliza Freytag Ayers, the benefactor, met the Reverend William A. Passavant, who was renowned for founding both orphanages and hospitals. Thus, what was to become Passavant Area Hospital, a landmark medical facility, was born.

Ayers donated a very valuable five-acre parcel of land on the most popular street in the city of Jacksonville for a medical facility that was originally named Jacksonville Hospital. When the hospital opened in 1875, two deaconesses, Sister Louisa Marthens and Sister Caroline Ochse, managed the day-to-day operations of the hospital. Both were from the motherhouse in Kaiserswerth, Germany, where Florence Nightingale had trained. The deaconesses were the major source of nursing until the nursing school was established in 1902.

When the Reverend Passavant died in 1894, in recognition of his benevolence and dedication to the hospital, the facility was renamed Passavant Memorial Hospital. According to Dorothea L. Dix, the eminent philanthropist and director of nursing in Civil War Hospitals, Reverend Passavant was "one of those men of rare power, Fenelon-like spirit, and Apostolic self-sacrifice, whom we occasionally see rising up to show the astonished world how much one man can accomplish through the force of moral power, without riches, save the riches of a sanctified spirit."

In 1953, after it was determined rising material and labor costs would prohibit the renovation of the original hospital on East State, a new 140-bed facility was opened at the current location on West Walnut Street. The new hospital was erected on farmland donated by Charles A. Rowe, in memory of his parents.

Through numerous changes since 1953, Passavant Area Hospital has remained steadfast in its commitment to offer innovative leadership in improving the health of the people it serves by providing excellent care, guided by compassion and individualized service.

Passavant Area Hospital offers a total healthcare campus. The fully accredited hospital includes an education complex, physician's offices, an emergency department and Level II Trauma Center, newly remodeled Maternal Infant Health Center, Transitional Care Unit, and a new Rehabilitation Services Building.

In addition to the invaluable contribution of excellent healthcare, Passavant's employees, volunteers, and physicians participate in numerous fundraising events in the area. The American Heart Association Heart Walk, the National MS Society Walk, the Cancer Relay for Life, elementary and high school sports programs, the Jacksonville Symphony Christmas Concert and a children's production at the Jacksonville Theatre Guild are but a few examples of Passavant's involvement in community service.

According to President and CEO Chester A. Wynn, "our challenge over the next few years is to keep building on our past successes so that Passavant Area Hospital maintains its leadership role in healthcare while continuing its history of service and caring for all—Friends caring for friends."

✧

Above: Passavant Hospital today.

Below: Reverend William A. Passavant, founder of Passavant Hospital.

VILLAGE OF ORLAND PARK

The Village of Orland Park certainly has come a long way from its days of horse drawn covered buggies, mail delivery from a stagecoach, and serving as an assembly point for cattle drives.

While Orland Park has evolved in pretty similar fashion to other towns, it has, however, in the past few decades emerged as a leader and one of the most dynamic southwest suburban Chicago areas.

The Orland area's rich history spans more than 26,000 years reaching far back into a time when glaciers covered the land and below the ice was abundantly rich with vegetation, wildlife, rivers and streams.

Eventually the area's ice gave way to farmers and other settlers who pioneered Orland Park's modest beginnings in the 1880s. It was at this time that railways were constructed through the area, and a few retail stores opened, including general stores, a furniture store, a blacksmith, creamery, a wagon shop and two saloons. Soon afterwards, a post office opened, along with the Orland Hotel and more businesses.

Orland Park's early development is humble compared to its progress over the centuries but one characteristic has remained. It was considered a market town in the nineteenth century, an important component in progress because the railroad gave it access to Chicago's markets as well. Today, Orland Park can still be called a market town, although it is no longer dependent upon the big city's markets.

The early 1900s saw a population of less than 350 people, a number that now equates to less than the population of one of the village's junior high schools. Growth continued, but at a rather slow pace throughout the next few decades.

Those who lived in Orland Park, however, always had plenty of recreational opportunities, a claim that still holds true today. There was the Orland Park Band for those who enjoyed making music and the upstairs to Creer's store where young people enjoyed dancing to the music played on a phonograph. People of all ages enjoyed baseball, America's favorite pastime, whether it was a friendly game between boys in a nearby vacant lot, or a men's team like the Orland Greys who played against other local towns. In the 1920s and 1930s, golf was becoming a very popular pastime and those from the area, as well as from Chicago, came to Orland Park to shoot a round at Silver Lake Country Club or nearby Palos Country Club and Gleneagles Country Club.

Although the population didn't grow at a fast pace at this time, many new "firsts" and new inventions were making their way into Orland Park. Electricity began lighting up the village in 1922 and the change from gas-fueled streetlights to electric lamps paved the way for newer, more modern appliances like refrigerators, washing machines, stoves and radios. At this time, the number of horses

on the roads began to diminish with the introduction of automobiles. Soon there were paved roads.

"Crystal sets," which required ear pieces so only one person at a time could hear the music, were replaced by radios, thus allowing entire families to sit together and enjoy music and other entertaining programs. Around the same time there was only one telephone company in Orland Park. Those who had a crank phone or a later model need only call the operator and ask to be connected to a desired party.

Major growth started to appear in the 1950s and has continued for decades. Developers back then, just as now, found Orland Park an attractive site for residential developments. Hence the first subdivision in Orland Park was built. The Orland Park Hills subdivision offered three-bedroom homes with one bathroom and an attached one-car garage for less than $20,000.

In 1955, Orland Park voters approved a bond issue to finance water system improvements that would ensure an adequate supply for this growing community. Four years later, water and sewerage systems were expanded to handle a population of 8,000 people, four times more than its population of 2,000 people at that time. Once this and other infrastructure was in place, Orland Park became one of the most sought-after areas in southwest Cook County.

Thanks to the foresight of the founding fathers and continued responsible management by elected officials and an appointed administrative team, Orland Park continues to be at the forefront and is considered a role model to many other communities because of its proactive and positive approach.

Under the direction of Mayor Daniel McLaughlin and the board of trustees, Orland Park's commercial community continues to thrive thanks to their numerous programs designed to attract and retain business.

Home sales continue to be brisk and new residential developments with luxurious homes are raising the standard of the quality of life in Orland Park.

Delighted with the prosperity that comes along with the growth, but concerned that Orland Park's precious natural resources would be gone, Mayor McLaughlin created the Open Lands of Orland Park. To date, nearly three hundred acres of land have been donated to and/or purchased by the village in an attempt to preserve some of Orland Park's open spaces from future development. It is these open spaces and green beltways, combined with hundreds of acres of forest preserves and a great park system that are at the top of the list of why people choose Orland Park to make their home.

Residents also continue to enjoy the finest in recreational facilities that offer an abundance of outdoor and indoor recreational opportunities for all ages and abilities. There are more than forty neighborhood and community parks equipped with ball fields, picnic areas, playground equipment and more. Plus there is a state-of-the-art Skate Park and an aquatic center that surpasses all others when it comes to family fun. The newest addition to the recreational facilities is the Sportsplex, a multiuse facility that offers numerous additional recreational opportunities.

Orland Park is also fortunate to have an award-winning police department that helps to ensure the public's safety and takes a positive and proactive approach to crime prevention. Municipal services are second to none and officials work on a daily basis to meet the needs and demands of this dynamic community. An outstanding fire protection district also serves the population, complete with the most up-to-date emergency equipment.

All the while Orland Park continues its progress by offering an exemplary school system, access to the finest healthcare facilities, proximity to major highways, a diverse spiritual community, a myriad of shopping and dining establishments, a wide range of housing choices, and the finest in recreational opportunities.

The progress continues but not without a concerted effort on the part of many to preserve its historically rich past, a component vital to its future.

VILLAGE
OF
ORLAND PARK

BRANDT CONSOLIDATED

Since the years following World War II, Illinois agriculture has gone through profound technological changes. One of Central Illinois' pioneers in the custom fertilizer business is Brandt's Fertilizer Service, which was organized in 1953 by Glen Brandt and his sister, Evelyn Brandt Thomas, with one product—anhydrous ammonia—and one truck. In 1957 the company's headquarters were built in Pleasant Plains, Illinois. Today, Brandt has ten retail locations in Central Illinois with over 2,000 customers and an array of more than 200 products including a complete line of fertilizers, seed, feed, herbicides and propane. In addition to its core custom application of fertilizers and herbicides, Brandt's has expanded its scope to other services—GPS receivers, yield monitors, and state-of-the-art technology. The company serves as a one-stop shop for farmers. The next generation of Brandt's assumed leadership of the company in 1995 when Rick Brandt, son of Glen Brandt, was named CEO and president.

In 1967 the wholesale chemical and micronutrient division known as Brandt Chemical was created. It was split into two divisions: The Dealer Support Division and ClawEl Specialty Products. The Dealer Support Division offers other retailers the same fertilizer products, decision support systems and technical support given to Brandt's own customers. The ClawEl division manufactures micronutrient, adjuvants, specialty fertilizers and turf nutrients for a worldwide market including the United States, Mexico, South America, Europe, and the Middle East. Customers include citrus growers, vegetable growers, nurseries and golf courses.

Today, computers have removed much of the guesswork from farming. Brandt offers its High Q Decision Support system to farmers seeking precision agricultural information to use in crop planning. Growers enrolled in the program enter site-specific crop input data, along with soil and climate information into a laptop computer provided by Brandt's that is connected to a global positioning satellite receiver. The information is then analyzed to help farmers with input decisions.

In 1990, Brandt's Fertilizer Service and Brandt Chemical were merged to form Brandt Consolidated. Today, Brandt Consolidated is a full service fertilizer company with three divisions: Retail Fertilizer, Dealer Support and ClawEl Specialty Products.

Customer service and satisfaction is an important part of the success of Brandt Consolidated. The company trains and develops employees to be knowledgeable of the latest in profitable technologies and how customers can best use them. Over 150 people are working hard to keep Brandt on the cutting edge of information and technology.

With fifty years of experience behind it, Brandt Consolidated has become a leader in the agricultural community worldwide and will continue its leadership role in seeking out new technologies and opportunities for its customer's advantage.

DEERE & COMPANY

When John Deere fashioned his self-scouring steel plow in 1837, he revolutionized agriculture and laid the foundation for Deere & Company, the world's leading manufacturer of agricultural and forestry equipment. From his first plow to his last, John Deere settled for only the highest standards of quality for his implements. This tradition continues today with employees who faithfully follow his legacy of quality, innovation, integrity, and commitment. Deere & Company is the oldest major manufacturer in the state of Illinois.

In 1836, John Deere left his home and family in Vermont and established a blacksmith shop in the community of Grand Detour, near Dixon, Illinois. He soon learned that though the soil of the Prairie State was rich and fertile, it was difficult to till using the cast-iron plows common at the time. With great ingenuity, John Deere cut and shaped a steel moldboard and created a plow with a highly polished surface that allowed the soil to slide right off. Deere's blacksmith shop soon was turning out dozens of plows every year, and by 1842 manufacturing exceeded over one hundred plows annually. Deere relocated to Moline, Illinois, in 1848 because of its excellent transportation facilities and waterpower, and the company has been headquartered there ever since. Within a few years, production reached sixteen hundred plows per year.

John's son Charles joined the firm in 1853, taking over management of the company

several years later, after it narrowly avoided bankruptcy. While plows remained the principal product, other farm implements were being developed and marketed.

The company continually introduced improved models of plows and cultivators in the 1860s. The name Deere & Company appeared in 1868 after the firm incorporated. In the 1870s, Deere & Company pioneered the sulky plow and two-row corn planter. Before he died in 1886 at the age of eighty-two, John Deere saw his company expand to include five dominant product lines: plows, cultivators, harrows, drills and planters, and wagons and buggies. These products were marketed through sales branches in five major cities.

By the early twentieth century, Deere & Company had become a major manufacturer of mechanized farm machinery. Charles Deere remained the company's president until his death in 1907, when his son-in-law, William Butterworth, assumed his role.

Under Butterworth's direction, the company underwent a major reorganization. By 1912 the firm consisted of twelve manufacturing entities and twenty-five sales organizations in the United States and Canada. The company entered the tractor business in 1918 with the purchase of the Waterloo Gasoline Engine Company. The popular Model D tractor was introduced five years later. Deere

Above: Company founder John Deere was an inventive and skilled blacksmith who also served as the second mayor of Moline in 1873.

Below: Tour the John Deere Historic Site in Grand Detour, and see the exact location of the original blacksmith shop and visit John Deere's home.

& Company began manufacturing harvesters in 1913 and introduced its first combine in 1927. William Butterworth relinquished control to family member Charles Deere Wiman who ran it until 1955.

Farm practices changed during this time as increasing mechanization led to larger farms and Deere continued to adapt to the new market. At the beginning of the Great Depression, Deere & Company was one of only seven full-line equipment manufacturers left in the country. The company strengthened its customer loyalty during this time by carrying debtor farmers as long as necessary. The 1940s were a decade of great innovation as several new developments in machinery were introduced: the four-row tractor-drawn planter, self-propelled combine, automatic wire-tie bailer, and the first diesel tractor.

The last representative of the Deere family, William A. Hewitt, became the chief executive officer in 1955 following the death of his father-in-law Charles Deere Wiman. Hewitt led the company until 1982. With a decision to build a small tractor assembly plant in Mexico and purchase a controlling interest in a German tractor company, Deere & Company became a multinational manufacturer. The company continued to expand its presence into other countries in the next few years. Deere's first real industrial tractor, the 440 crawler, was introduced in 1958, and marked

the company's rise to a position as a leading manufacturer of construction equipment in the United States. John Deere Credit was created at this time as well.

In the 1960s, Deere & Company diversified into new markets with the manufacture of consumer goods including lawn and garden tractors and ventured into the forestry equipment industry as well. During this time company officials created the John Deere Insurance Group. The company surpassed International Harvester as the world's largest producer and seller of farm and industrial tractors during this period of rapid expansion. This growing diversification led to the company's reorganization into three major divisions in 1970. The 1980s proved to be a challenging time period for the company because of a long-lasting downturn in the farm economy which depressed equipment sales. Deere & Company was able to weather this storm and return to profitability. A new division, John Deere Health Care Incorporated, was created in 1985 and promised to become a major healthcare provider.

The firm was restructured in the 1990s into the four separate operating divisions that exist today. Deere & Company is poised to continue its global growth through key acquisitions, introduction of innovative technology, and by providing quality products to its customers.

From a one-man blacksmith shop building a revolutionary steel plow, Deere & Company has grown over the past 168 years to become a multinational corporation providing a wide range of products to customers in more than 160 countries. With over forty-six thousand employees worldwide, the company's success continues to be driven by the same principles of highest quality laid down by its founder.

✧

Above: The John Deere Pavilion in downtown Moline is celebrated as the most comprehensive agricultural exhibit in the world, with displays of both vintage and current equipment.

Below: One of the largest and most advanced facilities in the John Deere family is located in Illinois. At the John Deere Harvester Works in East Moline, agricultural combines are built-to-order to customer specifications.

THE FARMERS BANK OF LIBERTY

The history of The Farmers Bank of Liberty and its surrounding territory are virtually inseparable, as the bank's assets and employees have played an integral part in the development of Liberty and surrounding communities for over a hundred years. From the installation of electricity and phone services, to the attraction of a state highway and the creation of a four-year high school, the directors, officers and staff of The Farmers Bank of Liberty have labored for the long-term growth and well being of the area they serve.

Through prosperity and adversity; wars, recessions and the Great Depression; and even three bank robberies in its colorful past, The Farmers Bank of Liberty still stands as a monument of responsible helpfulness to its patrons. Local deposits, which are an investment in the community by the community, have remained at home to help build successful farming enterprises and prosperous businesses throughout the area, and to make available affordable loans for housing, automobiles and other consumer durable goods. No other investment can yield as much "total return" for the community.

On June 23, 1903, business and civic leaders of Liberty (located in Adams County, just to the West of Quincy) gathered together in order to establish a bank to serve the growing financial needs of the community and the surrounding area. The bank was originally chartered as the Farmers State Bank

of Liberty. However, the original charter was surrendered back to the state and The Farmers Bank of Liberty was reorganized as a private bank in 1904—all without any interruptions in service to the community.

The bank was originally located on the ground floor of the Masonic Hall in Liberty. When a new building was erected in 1913, a community hall, later known as the "Opera House" was built on the second floor. In 1972 the bank's board decided to construct a new facility at the bank's present location. A major remodeling and expansion was completed on the main banking house in 2003, just in time for the bank's hundredth anniversary celebration.

To illustrate the symbiotic development of the bank and its community, one need only read the board meeting minutes, which are intact yet today. In 1914 the minutes reflected that Bank Cashier Stephen G. Lawless and a Dr. Lierly employed the L. H. Richardson Company to survey a direct route from Liberty to Quincy for an "auto interurban." In July of 1915, a committee of the board was appointed to "investigate an electric light plant" for the village, and in 1926, a resolution was adopted asking for priority in construction of Illinois Route 105, now known as Route 104, which serves as Main Street to the village of Liberty. Providing for infrastructure improvements for a growing community remains a priority with the bank, with new subdivisions and other developments being solicited and financed today.

Innovative. Progressive. Creative. This is how the bank looks at serving the financial needs of the community. From the first safety deposit box, which could be rented for $1.50 per year, to the latest in check imaging and

✧

Above: The Farmers Bank of Liberty started operations on June 23, 1903 in the first floor of the Masonic Lodge in Liberty.

Below: The main "banking facility" at 1002 North Main Street in Liberty. A major remodeling and expansion of this facility was completed just before the bank's hundredth anniversary in 2003.

leading edge products and services, The Farmers Bank has provided a complete range of financial services to its customers throughout its history. Today, the bank offers a wide variety of checking, savings, retirement plans and loans, and to further serve all of the financial needs of area customers, a full service insurance agency, Hometown Insurance Services, Inc., was added to the Liberty facility in late 2003. After the branching laws in Illinois would allow it, a full service banking facility was built in nearby Barry, Illinois in 1995 and a small branch in Payson, Illinois was purchased and remodeled in 1998, both of which have experienced a good rate of growth in their own right. This has helped the bank recognize more of its natural trade area and has made banking more convenient for its rural customer base.

Ownership of the bank has been held in local hands throughout most of its history. In 1972 the local stockholders voted to sell the bank to a gentleman from Olympia Fields, Illinois. In 1976, Kurt Schaffer of Kewanee, Illinois purchased the majority interest from Drovers Bank, which had taken over the bank stock. Schaffer agreed to sell his stock in 1984 to a former associate, Robert R. Field who was named president and vice-chairman at that time. Field's son, Mark joined the bank in 1985 as a loan officer and immediately began to buy out the minority shareholders, until all of the bank's stock was owned by father and son. Mark was named president in early 1990 at the age of twenty-six. The elder Field retired in 1992 and sold his remaining

interest to his son but stayed on the bank's board until 1995 when Mark was then elected to the additional post of chairman of the board. Mark is a past president of the Community Bankers Association of Illinois and is also active in the Independent Community Bankers of America. Mark hopes that his children, Christie and Bobby, will someday show an interest in becoming a proud small-town community banker as well.

From its humble beginnings in 1903, The Farmers Bank of Liberty has become an important fixture in the long-term growth and well being of the communities it serves, as its assets have grown from $10,000 in 1903 to over $45 million currently. Its formula for success lies in its commitment to its founding ideals—to be a locally owned, real community bank with strong, civic-minded officers and staff who have a burning desire to help the communities they serve to become great places to raise a family and to grow a business!

❖

Above: The bank's first branch office was constructed in 1995 on Highway 106 in Barry, just off of Interstate 72.

Below: The Payson branch on Highway 96 was purchased and remodeled in 1998.

St. Louis-based Ameren Corporation's three Illinois utilities—AmerenCIPS, AmerenCILCO and AmerenIP—have provided reliable electric and natural gas service to central and southern Illinois for more than a century. But until the late 1990s, the name "Ameren" didn't even exist.

Ameren Corporation was formed in 1997 with the merger of Union Electric Company (UE) and CIPSCO Incorporated, parent company of Central Illinois Public Service Company (CIPS)—now AmerenCIPS. The company grew in 2003 with the acquisition of CILCORP Inc., parent company of Central Illinois Light Company (CILCO), now AmerenCILCO, and again in 2004 with the acquisition of Illinois Power Company (IP), now AmerenIP.

Each of these proud companies was founded to provide needed public services. Each would grow to become industry leaders in the increasingly vital—and competitive—electric and natural gas industry. And together, they would come to serve nearly two million customers in Illinois—sixty percent of Ameren's 3.2-million customer base—and represent a fascinating era of Illinois history.

In 1902, CIPS' predecessor, Mattoon City Railway, incorporated to provide streetcar service in Mattoon. Two years later, CIPS acquired the electric generating plant and distribution system in Mattoon. In 1912 it became a subsidiary of Middle West Utilities Company, operating an electric light and power business in the cities of Mattoon, Charleston and Kansas.

CIPS soon acquired sixty public service areas, and over the next several years, the company planned and constructed transmission lines connecting the various towns in its territory. In its first twelve years,

the company that started as one streetcar line and one city electric plant soon had eight generating stations—with 11 in reserve—serving 232 communities.

In the late 1920s and early 1930s, CIPS linked its power lines to several communities served by IP and contracted for power with the Missouri General Utilities Company.

In 1934, CIPS introduced natural gas to the remaining interconnected area previously supplied with manufactured gas, making gas service available to ninety-five percent of its electric customers.

CIPS began building power plants in Illinois in the 1940s. By the end of the decade, CIPS had ceased to be a subsidiary of the Middle West Corp., and the company was selling or closing many of its ice properties and other businesses. By the end of 1951, the company was engaged only in electric and gas public utility services.

The 1960s' growth in customers and electrical service demand meant new plants and updates to existing plants. By 1979 the company had constructed five coal-fired plants generating 2,900 megawatts of electricity. When the company merged with UE in 1997, it served 323,000 electric customers and 169,000 natural gas customers in 557 Illinois communities.

CILCO's story begins nearly a half-century before that of CIPS. In 1853 the Peoria Light & Coke Company began manufacturing and selling gas in the City of Peoria. Thirty years later, the Jenny Electric Light & Power Company organized to build electric lines in the city, purchasing its power from Illinois Electric Power Company in East Peoria. In 1889 the company constructed Liberty Street Station, becoming its own generator of power.

Between 1911 and 1913, a series of mergers involving Peoria Light & Coke, Jenny Electric Light & Power and other gas and electric companies formed CILCO. The fledgling company provided gas, electric and steam energy to Peoria and twenty-six surrounding communities and began building power plants to meet the growing need for electricity.

The company's first steam electric plant was the R. S. Wallace station, built in the mid-1920s and expanded in the late 1930s and early 1940s. Other plants would follow, notably E. D. Edwards in 1957 and Duck Creek in 1976.

Over the next several years, CILCO constructed two major gas lines and the first section of a 69,000-volt underground cable in Peoria to provide natural gas and electricity to more than one hundred communities in the Peoria, Springfield and Lacon areas, and steam heat to the central business districts of Peoria and Springfield.

Like many utilities, the 1990s presented new challenges for CILCO. Increased competition for energy services from independent power producers resulted in new strategies to secure long-term power-supply agreements. In 1994 the company became the first electric utility and the second natural gas utility worldwide to earn Quality Assured Supplier Status from Caterpillar, Inc., headquartered in Peoria.

As AmerenCILCO, the company today serves 203,000 electric and 208,000 natural gas customers in a 4,500 square-mile area of central and east-central Illinois.

Like CIPS and CILCO, IP was born when various public service companies combined forces. In 1923 the Illinois Traction System and the Southern Illinois Light and Power Co. merged to form Illinois Power and Light Corp.

Also like CIPS and CILCO, the young IP was more than an electric and gas utility. It also provided steam heat, water service, door-to-door ice delivery and even bus and interurban streetcar transportation services—allowing the company to survive the Great Depression. However, before the start of World War II, demand for electricity and natural gas service eclipsed IP's other businesses. By 1940 the company claimed nearly 222,000 electric and 95,000 natural gas customers. Less than two

decades later, the company had built major generating stations in Havana, Wood River, Vermilion and Hennepin, and it had invested in several large-capacity natural gas storage fields.

On December 1, 1952, IP, CIPS and UE linked their power transmission system operations, allowing the companies to operate with less generation, make maximum use of the most efficient generating plants, provide emergency energy to each other and install larger, more efficient generating units.

Throughout the 1960s, Illinois Power continued to add generating units, including Baldwin Plant, the company's largest generating facility. By the end of the decade, the company's electric customer count had nearly doubled and its natural gas customers had tripled.

The joint agreement between IP, CIPS and UE foreshadowed the cooperation that would take place between the companies in the decades to follow. In 1978, IP crews came to the rescue of Union Electric during a devastating ice storm, and UE returned the favor in 1986.

IP, CIPS and CILCO played vital roles in restructuring the state's utility laws in the 1990s. The resulting Customer Choice Law opened the door to choice for Ameren's commercial, industrial and residential customers in Illinois.

Restructuring also brought change, as these utilities sold their electricity generating plants and became integrated distribution companies.

As part of Ameren Corporation, AmerenCIPS, AmerenCILCO and AmerenIP are even better positioned to continue fulfilling their commitment to reliably delivering energy to the citizens of Illinois.

✧

Opposite, top: These CILCO employees demonstrate the proper use, care, and feeding of the turn-of-the-century version of the utility truck.

Opposite, bottom: In the 1950s, Illinois Power marketed everything from stoves and refrigerators to vacuum cleaners and electric lamps, which it sold door-to-door.

Above: Throughout its hundred-year history, Ameren's equipment certainly has changed, but not its commitment to service.

Below: When completed in 1931, the CIPS headquarters building in downtown Springfield was the largest office building in the state outside of Chicago.

Freedom Oil
Company

From life on a farm, to a $5-a-week bookkeeper at a bank, to the bank presidency, financial devastation in the 1929 market crash, renewed wealth from a career switch to farm machinery sales, then another to building and operating a bus to aid the war effort—one of the most successful, independent oil companies in the country has evolved. One remarkable man started the evolution.

By the time Frank S. Owens was introduced to the petroleum industry, as his bus hauled gasoline along with local residents to their jobs at the Elmwood Ordnance Plant at the height of World War II, he had experienced the extreme highs, lows, twists and turns of a business executive's career during the volatile 1920s and 1930s. Widely recognized for his financial and business acumen as the leader of a Kokomo bank and an automobile dealership, he lost everything with the market crash and collapse of the financial industry. In the early '40s, now highly successful at selling farm machinery, the imaginative Owens saw opportunity and a chance at meaningful wartime service by building a 35-passenger bus with a used body and an enlarged tractor frame. Times were very tough, local citizens needed a way to get to work at the defense plant in Joliet (converted from a farm implement manufacturer), and there wasn't a bus to be found anywhere.

"It wasn't fancy, but it never let us down," Owens recalled. The bus ended up traveling almost half a million miles over central Illinois highways. Hauling gasoline for the Wood River Refining Company led to Frank Owens' fourth, and last, career change. He bought a string of ten small service stations, owned by T. G. Wells of Decatur. The enterprise that was to become Owens Oil Company, and later Freedom Oil Company, had been launched.

There were problems with Owens' new business, including a shortage of able-bodied men due to the war's manpower drain, and continued gas rationing. But with the able assistance of Clarence Cruslus, a former member of the Wells Organization, the company progressed rapidly, profits grew, and the original purchase price was paid off in less than three years.

Over the next two decades Owens Oil grew into a remarkably successful company. Although Frank Owens preferred not to be specific about growth figures, he once stated, "just say we have had about a fifty-fold increase in twenty years." He attributed much of the company's success to cultivating a distinctly favorable public image, utilizing "home grown talent" for station managers, and concentrating on fast, friendly service.

In 1968, Frank Owens passed away, the company had been sold to Clark Oil

Company, and Arnold Owens, Frank's son and vice president of Owens Oil, was looking into new ventures. He had accumulated eight gasoline stations, including five in Florida, and the Florida stations were to become the cornerstone of the second generation of the Owens Oil family gasoline business. Arnold Owens, Inc. grew to twelve locations by the mid 1970s, and in order to obtain more gasoline during the gas shortage of those years, Arnold purchased a Texaco bulk plant. Shortly thereafter he formed a new corporation—Freedom Oil.

During the 1970s, with the help of his children, Arnold was instrumental in developing a new but dynamic trend in America—convenience stores. Self-service allowed gasoline marketers to add additional profit centers to their locations by selling items such as milk, soda, cigarettes, snacks, and beer. By the early 1980s the business had grown to over twenty locations. By 1995, when Arnold passed away, his strong leadership had resulted in the operation of thirty-five stores and over 30 million gallons in annual gasoline sales. Three of his children had joined him at Freedom Oil.

Arnold Owens supreme dedication to his family and church, his philosophy of being ready for each and every day, and his motto of, "Don't give up! Don't quit! Treat every day as a new experience to learn from," left a very positive and lasting impression with the employees of Freedom Oil. His dynamic leadership advanced the company into the twenty-first century and established a firm

framework for future success. His broad smile and contagious laugh is fondly remembered.

Today, Freedom Oil owns and operates fifty retail gasoline convenience stores in central Illinois and Florida, operates five gasoline transports, and sells wholesale gasoline to many branded and independent dealer accounts. The company sells over 50 million gallons of gasoline products annually and has revenues in excess of $125 million.

Michael Owens, currently the president of Freedom Oil, states, "the only constant in the gasoline business over the three generations and sixty years the Owens family has been in it, is change." Freedom Oil Company has certainly proved the motto "change is good." But according to Michael, even though Freedom will continue to adapt to compete in an ever-evolving market place, the company will always have a steadfast commitment to its longstanding mission statement:

To provide consistently high quality products and dependable services, at a competitive cost, with friendliness, efficiency and responsibility, to our customers, our employees, our families, and the communities we serve.

Currently, all six of Arnold Owens' children are either officers or board members of Freedom Oil. There are twelve grandchildren. It will soon be time for the fourth generation to decide if they want to step into roles that will keep the family business alive and well for many years to come.

PALMER HOUSE HILTON

Synonymous with the elegance and glitter of Chicago, the Palmer House Hilton has been a leading attraction for visitors on Chicago's lakefront for over 135 years. Located in the heart of the city's cultural, business and financial center, just minutes from major interstate expressways and railroads, with at-the-door shuttle service to both O'Hare and Midway Airports, this grand beauty from another era has been stunningly restored to its original breathtaking opulence and remains one of only twenty-six grand palace hotels in America today.

Founded by leading businessman Potter Palmer in 1871, the hotel's first building, destroyed by the Great Chicago Fire, literally rose from the ashes with a magnificent replacement that became a social gathering place in the new city. Its eighty-five foot bar and barber shop floor inlaid with silver dollars became Chicago legends. United States Presidents Garfield and Cleveland held famous public receptions at the Palmer House and President Ulysses S. Grant was entertained there by Mark Twain. Palmer had been responsible for the development of State Street. He raised the street level in the downtown area and created North Lake Shore Drive by pushing the lake back and later building his family mansion there. When the present hotel building was being constructed in 1925 guests remained in one half of the old building and, when the new half was complete, were moved to new quarters in one hour. Afterward the remaining section of the old building was demolished.

The spectacular lobby ceiling is the first of the Palmer House's art treasures to greet guests. Commissioned by Palmer's wife, Bertha Honore, the ceiling is made up of twenty-one individual paintings created by noted nineteenth century French muralist Louis Pierre Rigal in the style of the High French Empire period. On the occasion of the hotel's 125th anniversary in 1996, Lido Lippi, Italian art restorer with an international reputation, restored these. Here too are displayed other stunning art treasures including the bronze sculpture of Romeo and Juliet and pair of Winged Golden Angels by Louis C. Tiffany, a silver case with some of the original silver pieces used by President Ulysses S. Grant, Mark Twain, Buffalo Bill and other nineteenth century notables and Palmer House luminaries. Additionally, displays of Mrs. Palmer's fine twenty-two-karat gold, French porcelain Haviland china service is housed in its own case.

Concurrent with the opening of the 1933 World's Fair, Chicago's Palmer House management opened the celebrated Empire Room for visitors. Decorated to reflect the French Empire period, the glamorous gathering spot is awash in brilliant colors, green and gold mirrors and a lavish, gold leaf

ceiling. French-made chandeliers of crystal and gold, with ostrich plume motif, crown the room with its gold reliefs of Napoleon and Josephine. This regal reception room has been called "the most beautiful public space in Chicago." Here entertainers Carol Channing, Pearl Bailey, Tony Bennett, Jimmy Durante, Nat "King" Cole, Louis Armstrong, Maurice Chevalier, and a host of others have entertained audiences. Today the Empire Room is home to Chicago's most elegant private parties.

An arcade of shops features a blend of the old and the new. Marble and glass storefronts house exclusive shops, offering jewelry, art, novelties, and drug and sundry items. The Big Downtown, newest of the hotel's eateries, joins the famed Trader Vic's and the French Quarter.

Although the Palmer House Hilton wears comfortably the dignity of age, it is entirely contemporary in service and quality. A renovation program of seven years duration saw complete remodeling of 1639 guest rooms, installation of a state-of-the-art heating and air conditioning system, computerized check-in/check-out system and a seventh floor multi-functional center. With over 1,600 guest rooms, 88 suites, and 11 room Penthouse Suite, there are accommodations for every need. The warm, traditional décor of every room is welcoming and relaxing. Guests have access to the pool and complete fitness club, with professional staff.

With Chicago's reputation as America's leading convention city, the Palmer House Hilton provides a complete business and service center on the seventh floor. Conference Center Seven is a four million dollar complex tailored to small meetings and offers a wide range of options. Meetings from 6 to 100 people can be accommodated in the 40,000-square-foot complex with its 38 custom meeting rooms and 6 distinct areas or "wings." First quality furnishings provide a dignified backdrop as well as comfort and functional arrangements for meetings. A complete, separate food and beverage service, concierge and lounges facilitate seamless meeting arrangements. State-of-the-art audio-visual equipment and a resident expert are available. Conference Center seven's dedicated staff, facilities and numerous support services are at the service of the traveling business or professional executive. It is the

largest, self-contained conference center in a major Chicago convention hotel.

The beauty of the hotel is known far and wide. When Conrad N. Hilton purchased the Palmer House for twenty million dollars in 1945, the hotel entered its present era and millions have been spent since in preserving this luxurious institution from a more lavish time. The Palmer House Hilton's grand lobby was the centerpiece for an *American Heritage* magazine story "America Invents the Grand Hotel." And grand indeed the hotel has remained. The name has been linked with elegance and first class accommodation throughout its long history and is today Chicago's oldest hotel and the longest continuously operating hotel in North America. Stay at the Palmer Hilton has always been a memorable experience.

✧

Opposite, bottom: One of the Palmer House Hilton's meeting rooms. It is part of Conference Center Seven; the extravagant business and service center located on the seventh floor.

Above: Inside a room at the luxurious Palmer House.

Below: The Empire Room's design mimics the decorating styles of the French Empire period. It is considered to be "the most beautiful public space in Chicago."

ALLSTATE

On a fall morning in 1930, as the 7:28 commuter train headed from Highland Park, Illinois for downtown Chicago, a suggestion was made to General Robert E. Wood, president and chairman of Sears, Roebuck & Company: Sears should start selling auto insurance by mail.

The country was deep into the Great Depression. Many long-term businesses were closing their doors at an alarming rate. General Wood, however, recognized that the automobile was fast becoming a mainstay of American life and an automobile insurance company was an opportunity to extend Sears services to the public. He convinced the Sears Board of Directors to finance this insurance company with $700,000.

With a name borrowed from an automobile tire sold in the Sears catalog, and the backing of Sears, the great adventure of Allstate Insurance Company began on April 17, 1931.

A tool-and-die maker from Aurora, Illinois, William Lehnertz became the first policyholder. By the end of 1931, Allstate had 4,217 policies in force, a premium volume of $118,323, twenty employees, and the beginnings of a great company.

At first, Allstate auto insurance was sold only by mail through the Sears catalog. But at the Chicago World's Fair in 1933, Allstate's first agent set up a card table in the corner of the big Sears exhibit and was immediately swamped with applications. By 1933, Allstate "booths" were popping up in Sears stores throughout the country.

As Sears expanded, Allstate expanded too. By 1939, just eight years after its birth, Allstate had 113,472 policyholders and 529 employees. That year alone, the company received 25,461 claims.

In the 1950s, Allstate began offering a "full circle of protection" in most states, introducing commercial fire, personal theft and home-owners, personal health and commercial liability, as well as boat owners policies. Agents spending full time in Sears stores began making appointments to visit homes or businesses of insurance prospects, and some agents were assigned to sales offices separate from Sears stores.

Throughout its seventy-year history, Allstate has cut its own path in the insurance industry—a path that many insurers subsequently followed:

In 1939, Allstate startled the industry by tailoring auto rates by age, mileage and use of car. The plan was so popular, the industry followed suit.

- In 1947, Allstate created an Illustrator Policy that used simpler language and illustrations to make it easier for customers to understand their policies.
- Allstate opened the first Drive-in Claim Office in 1952, revolutionizing the way auto claims are handled.
- In 1959, Allstate became the first major insurance company to offer premium discounts specifically to owners of increasingly popular small autos.
- Also in that year, Allstate established a catastrophe claim plan to bring large

numbers of claim specialists into a catastrophe area immediately following a disaster.

• Allstate Motor Club, the first truly national motor club, was formed in 1961.

• In the 1970s, Allstate began an awareness program encouraging automakers to produce "tougher cars," including sturdier bumpers of uniform height, and continued its efforts to promote auto passenger safety via seat belts, air bags and anti-drunk driving campaigns.

From meager beginnings through its great successes, Allstate always puts a priority on helping to improve the communities it serves. In 1952 the company established The Allstate Foundation. Today, The Allstate Foundation funds more than 1,000 programs per year that focus on solving some of society's current challenges: creating safe and vital communities; fostering economic empowerment; and teaching tolerance, inclusion and diversity. In 2003 and 2004, The Allstate Foundation contributed more than $30 million to nonprofit organizations.

At a grassroots level, the "Helping Hands Program," formally organized in 1976, has mobilized more than seventy-five percent of Allstate employees to volunteer their time and talents working on community causes. Today, the Helping Hands Program is flourishing. Thousands of employees work shoulder to shoulder with community partners volunteering in soup kitchens, rehabbing parks, tutoring

children, spending time with seniors, and cleaning up vacant lots.

In 1982, Allstate became a part of the Sears Financial Network. And in 1993, Allstate became the largest publicly held insurance company when Sears sold 19.8 percent ownership of Allstate. At the time, it was the largest initial public offering (IPO) in history for a U.S. company. On June 30, 1995, Allstate became a totally independent company when Sears spun off the remaining eighty percent of Allstate to Sears' shareholders.

Allstate has come a long way since it began selling auto insurance in 1931. Today, Allstate is a *Fortune 500* company with $134 billion in assets, and is headquartered in Northbrook, Illinois. Allstate insures one out of every eight autos and homes in America and is one of the country's leading life insurers. Allstate helps people in more than 16 million households and offers retirement and investment products as well as banking services. Nearly 70,000 professionals support Allstate customers. Of our employees, twenty-nine percent are minorities and sixty percent are women. Allstate sells thirteen major lines of insurance, including auto, property, life and commercial.

For more information, please visit www.allstate.com.

❖

Above: In 1952, Allstate opened the first Drive-In claim office, revolutionizing the way auto claims were handled.

Below: The first Allstate ad in a Sears, Roebuck and Company publication appeared on this page in the 1932 Spring General Catalog.

THE FIRST NATIONAL BANK OF BARRY

For over a century The First National Bank of Barry has served the financial needs of the local community, persisting through wars, economic highs and lows, and dramatic advances in technology. The bank opened its doors on the first floor of the Masonic Building on May 1, 1901, with 3 employees, 26 shareholders, and $25,000 in capital.

The three-story Masonic Lodge in the Mortimer Street business district of Barry was built shortly after a devastating fire in 1894 razed much of the area. Initially the bank rented the first floor of the building, later buying it and the second floor, with the temple occupying the third floor. Today, The First National Bank of Barry still calls the Masonic Building home, but it has grown to hold over $16 million in capital, $110 million in assets, and has 36 shareholders, 10 of whom can trace their lineage back over a hundred years to the original 26. It offers a full range of banking services for both commercial and personal accounts. A trust department, providing complete trust services, was added in 1987.

From 1915 through 1917 the bank underwent a major renovation, which included the installation of a granite mosaic tile lobby floor, counters made from marble imported from the Island of Skyros in the Aegean Sea, a state-

of-the-art ladies' room and a new vault with a fire and burglar proof fourteen ton door. Just hauling the massive door from the train station to the bank and then moving it into place was a major engineering feat. The massive door was hauled on a wagon fitted with concrete wheels and pulled by an oil-powered tractor. Workmen had to remove a large portion of the building's south wall to get it in place. The door was moved in the 1980s during a renovation, when it was separated from its original wall and carted through the bank's lobby to its current home, guarding a newly constructed, expanded concrete vault. A fixture in Barry for over eighty years, this immense door is today a symbol of the security the bank has provided to the community since 1901.

The 1970s initiated a period of growth for The First National Bank of Barry, which continues through today. The renovation in 1972 included an addition that was built on the north side of the building to house the bookkeeping department and a new boardroom. Ten years later, a second addition was added for private offices, to enlarge the bookkeeping department and to move the boardroom. In 1992 a third addition was constructed to accommodate more private offices and to again enlarge the bookkeeping department, and relocate the boardroom.

❖

Above: The First National Bank of Barry established 1901, c.1917.

Below: In 1917 the vault door weighing fourteen tons was moved from the train station to the bank. The vault door was moved on a special trailer with concrete wheels and pulled by an oil-powered tractor.

In the bank's long history, there have been only five presidents, starting with Thomas A. Retallic in 1901; E. J. Stauffer in 1940; A. E. Vollbracht in 1968; and a year later with J. E. Gully. In 1996 John Shover took the reins as president after serving as CEO for the previous twenty-five years.

During Shover's tenure, assets of The First National Bank of Barry have increased from $3 million to $110 million. In order to keep up with the bank's increasing customer base, three new branches were opened in Pike and Adams Counties. The first branch, opened in Liberty in 1994, is located in a historic bank building, newly remodeled and designed to be efficient and modern, yet still retain its original style and décor. A motor banking branch with drive-up capabilities was opened in 1998 at the entrance of the Cieten development at Interstate 72's Exit 20. "I wanted to put in a drive-up facility, but there was no room here (at the main branch)," says Shover. "We bought the land at Cieten, where it's very accessible." The bank marked the new millennium with its latest addition, a Pittsfield branch, opened to better accommodate the many customers who live and work in that area.

The employees and shareholders of The First National Bank of Barry are proud to have served their loyal customers for over a century and are pleased with the contributions they have been able to make to their community's history. When the bank first opened its doors for business in 1901 their directors stated "To those who favor us with their patronage, we shall protect their interests," and that remains their pledge today.

For more information about The First National Bank of Barry, please visit www.fnbbarry.com.

❖

Above: A fixture in Barry since 1917, this massive but delicately machined vault door is a symbol of the security that The First National Bank of Barry has provided for a hundred years.

Below: The First National Bank of Barry located in its historic bank building.

INTERNATIONAL PROFIT ASSOCIATES, INC.

✦

The IPA Management Team. Standing (from left to right): Richard Atkinson, Shelle Bareck, Charles Botchway, Walt Master, Valerie Ramsdell, John Burgess, Ken Sweet, Scott Kollins, Andy Field, Nick Jones, and Tom Ryan. Sitting (from left to right): Rich Lubicz, Tyler Burgess, Katrin Owen, Gregg Steinberg, Robyn Barnett, Nick Karabas, and Tony Jones.

Buffalo Grove, a beautiful suburb just north of Chicago, is home to one of the most respected and fastest growing business development firms in the country. Founded by lawyer and former commodities trader John Burgess in 1991, International Profit Associates (IPA) and its sister company Integrated Business Analysis (IBA) have established themselves as the leading management consultancy for the owners of small- to medium-size businesses. IPA/IBA has never wavered in its commitment to its mission to improve the operations and enhance the profitability of companies headed by entrepreneurs.

IPA/IBA began with twenty-two employees and, within five years, saw a stunning 7,198 percent sales growth. IPA/IBA has helped to improve the operations of over one hundred thousand businesses and in 2003 had revenues of $182 million. Today, more than seventeen hundred employees throughout the United States and Canada offer a full range of business development services. The company is comprised of four main divisions: sales and marketing, analysis, consulting services, and valuations/mergers and acquisitions.

After the initial appointment is set, the analyst conducts a two to three day qualitative and quantitative analysis of each business. The process includes a comprehensive review of every component of the business including its management, operations, finances, controls, incentives, tax issues and more. The analyst listens to the owner's wants and needs, and evaluates trends within the company and within the industry. The process concludes with a detailed explanation of the findings, results and recommendations to address the owner's issues and concerns.

In essence, IPA/IBA holds a mirror up to the client defining his strengths and weaknesses, calculates their impact on profitability and helps to determine a course of action. From the snapshot of the business as it is and where it has been, IPA/IBA helps clients predetermine where they want to be and devises strategies to help the client get there. IPA/IBA shares the principles of success with its clients and in so doing transforms the owners and managers from technical experts into master strategists.

IPA/IBA distinguishes itself from other firms in many ways including its adherence to serving

its clients on a project basis rather than with a long-term retainer. The firm joins the team of its clients, working in conjunction with the owner and employees, to take the business to the next level of success and prosperity, while ensuring each client retains complete control over the work product on a daily basis.

Hailed as the leader in strengthening America's small- and medium-size businesses, company owners as well as political leaders have weighed in on the success of IPA/IBA. In December 1999, President George Bush said, "Businesses like IPA are generating the kinds of jobs and opportunities that we need to stay strong, providing the kinds of innovative services and products we need to stay productive."

In December 2001, President Bill Clinton celebrated the company's continued success, "Over the past eight years, during the longest economic expansion in American history, you grew faster than any management consulting company in history, and I congratulate you for that. And the small- and medium-size businesses that you helped to flourish fueled America's economic growth."

Small business owners have found IPA/IBA to be well versed in its knowledge and tireless in its desire to take businesses to the next level of productivity. Testimonials range from electric and communication companies to real estate and resource corporations. The president of Communitech, Inc. says, "IPA delivered tangible systems, procedures, and battle plans, which are already in place. They have handed back to me a new business with direction and purpose."

Business owners continually praise IPA as having given them the confidence to move forward and the tools to ensure the desired results. The owner of Whitakers, Inc., defines IPA/IBA's phenomenal work as "a vision, a plan…a direction towards profitability. I have found the compass."

That compass, an objective assessment and a second look at the inner workings of each business, is the specialty of International Profit Associates/Integrated Business Analysis. For more information about the company, its services and benefits, please visit www.ipa-iba.com.

✧

Top: John Burgess and President George Bush.

Middle: John Burgess and President Bill Clinton.

Bottom: Illinois Senator Dick Durbin and Dana and John Burgess.

HILTON CHICAGO

For over seventy-five years the Hilton Chicago has built upon its historic past and used modern conveniences to become one of the great landmark hotels of the Chicago skyline and remain one of the city's premier convention and meeting places.

Intrepid hotelier Conrad Hilton made a stylish entry into the Chicago hotel market when he purchased the renowned Stevens Hotel for $7.5 million in 1945. Hilton's growing chain of hotels already extended from coast to coast with the Roosevelt and Plaza in New York and the Townhouse in Los Angeles. The Stevens Hotel was a natural fit as Hilton expanded into the Chicago market. The twenty-eight story Stevens had earned a reputation far and wide as being the world's largest hotel when it opened in May 1927.

Its namesake owner, James W. Stevens, had a vision to build a hotel that offered the most extensive and complete convention facilities in the world. This gigantic undertaking, which cost $30 million to complete, created a virtual city within a city. The Stevens had 3,000 rooms, five sub-basements to house a power plant, a three-story laundry, all located on a full city block. For entertainment guests could take in a movie in the 1,200-seat theater, play golf on a eighteen-hole rooftop course, bowl, and ice skate, all within the confines of the building. Services included a private in-house hospital, barbershop, beauty shop and private fire and police forces.

With the coming of World War II, the United States Army, needing a large barracks, purchased the Stevens for $5 million. The grand hotel became one of the most luxurious barracks ever operated by the Army. Chicago contractor Stephen Healy bought the hotel in 1943 after one year of occupation by the military. Through his many contacts, Healy's organization was able to marshal enough materials to refurbish the hotel and reopen by November 1943 in wartime Chicago.

After Hilton's purchase, the name of hotel was changed to The Conrad Hilton Hotel in 1951. Hilton implemented many changes over the next few decades such as adding the Imperial North and South Suites in 1956, reducing and enlarging guest rooms from 3,000 to 2,200 in 1961 as well as building the Hilton Center Convention and Banquet Complex that same year. The hotel lobby was redesigned in 1968.

✧

Above: October 1, 1985, reopening after $185 million renovation.

Top, right: Mayor Richard J. Daley and Conrad Hilton escort Queen Elizabeth II in 1959.

Bottom: The magnificant exterior of the Hilton Chicago.

A major renovation was begun in 1984 and cost $185 million to complete, the largest hotel renovation in the world at this time. This final, major undertaking created the Hilton Chicago of today. The number of guest rooms was further reduced from 2,200 to 1,544. Guest rooms are richly appointed with classic cherry furnishings, many with two bathrooms complete with gleaming brass fixtures, exquisite Italian marble, high speed Internet access and Suite Dream Beds. Guests of the 209 executive class guest rooms are provided with a lavish array of personalized services plus a separate registration area and concierge. The 5,000-square-foot, Conrad Hilton Suite is one of thirteen specialty suites located on the tower-three and tower-four levels. This suite, which has hosted every United States' president since Ronald Reagan, features tapestry, lush custom-made carpets, chandeliers, a library with a bar and billiard table, hardwood floors and three balconies overlooking Lake Michigan and the city.

Other amenities created include a state-of-the-art fitness club, full-service business center, and over 243,000 square feet of exhibit space and over fifty meeting rooms. This enables the Hilton to handle the smallest meeting to extensive conventions and trade shows. Three new restaurants offer dining options from a signature steak house to an Irish Pub to All American dining.

Conveniently located on a full city block on South Michigan Avenue across from Grant Park, the Hilton is located just a few minutes walk or cab ride from virtually everything to see and do in Chicago. A leisurely stroll will take guests to many of Chicago's famous institutions including the Art Institute, Field Museum, Auditorium Theatre, and Symphony Center. Shoppers will also be glad to know that stores on North Michigan Avenue and State Street are only a few minutes walk away.

Every visitor to the Hilton Chicago will enjoy the luxurious and historic building and unparalleled service.

✧

Above: The Great Hall located inside of the Hilton Chicago.

Top, left: John F. Kennedy exiting the Michigan Avenue entrance of the Conrad Hilton.

Below: The Stevens' Family.

R. V. EVANS COMPANY

The R. V. Evans Company is one of the leading master distributors of flexible packaging, fastening and closure systems in the Midwest with a well-earned reputation as an innovator in offering solutions to the packaging and fastening challenges of its customers.

R. V. Evans, Sr., had been working as a manufacturer's representative since 1937 when, in 1951, he struck up a conversation with another salesman in the waiting room of a Decatur, Illinois manufacturer. That discussion changed Evans' future and laid the groundwork for a new company. In questioning the salesman about the small hand-held machine he was carrying, Evans learned that the device used metal staples to close corrugated cartons. Further inquiry led to an invitation to visit the manufacturing plant, Container Stapling Company, in Herrin, Illinois. Evans soon became a part-time distributor working out of his converted garage as a warehouse for the small quantities of product he carried while still maintaining his job as a manufacturer's representative of business forms.

This small operation followed with other product lines including those of the Paslode Company, a division of the Signode Steel Strapping Company. In 1962, while doing research for a hammer type-stapling machine capable of fastening paper lining in railroad boxcars, Evans located the Paslode Company, which manufactured the tool he needed. More

Above: R. V. Evans, Sr.

Below: The converted garage was used from 1941 to 1967 to warehouse small quantities of products. The garage was located at 2000 North Summit Avenue in Decatur, Illinois.

importantly, Paslode had a new pneumatic strip-nailing gun capable of placing nails into wood ten times faster than by hand. Evans added this line to his company and became one of fifty-four master distributors in the country to distribute this revolutionary nailing gun.

By the spring of 1963, Evans found that he could not handle all the work involved in running his business. He asked his son, R.V. "Dick" Evans, Jr., to consider resigning his teaching job in Taylorville, Illinois and join the growing firm. Dick started working for his father in June 1963. The younger Evans worked alongside his father beginning in the garage, handling the shipping and receiving of inventory, repairing/servicing of the tools, invoicing and calling on key customer contacts.

By 1968 the distributorship outgrew R. V.'s garage forcing them to purchase a four-thousand-square-foot building with a small truck dock on Logan Street in Decatur. R. V.'s second son, Tom, who had recently graduated from Eastern Illinois University with a degree in marketing, joined the firm. By this time, the company also employed two sales representatives. With their father nearing retirement age, the Evans brothers set about purchasing the business from him. The R.V. Evans Company was incorporated in 1970 with Dick Evans as president and Tom Evans as vice president.

Since that time R. V. Evans Company has added a wide range of quality product lines dealing with retail packaging, product protection, case closure, marking/labeling and unitizing/palletizing. The company has demonstrated its ability to learn the individual needs of its customers through an innovative problem solving technique. The company still offers nailing/stapling systems and specialty fastening systems to its customer base.

As a full service distributor, Evans' highly trained technical staff will install new pieces of equipment, train customer employees at their plant and repair tools and equipment as needed in one of three service locations.

The corporate sales and service center in Decatur has grown to approximately 40,000 square feet in two buildings. One houses the corporate offices, demonstration area and warehouse space and the other houses the company's service center. The R.V. Evans Company now serves a clientele base across five states in the Midwest: Iowa, Illinois, Kansas, Missouri and Nebraska. Two branch centers in Rockford, Illinois, and St. Louis, Missouri, help provide the necessary support for the R. V. Evans Company's many customers.

R. V. Evans Company currently employs sixty-two people in Decatur and its branch locations. Solid values and traditions have been passed down to the next generation of Evans family members. Kelly Evans, son of Dick Evans learned the business from the ground up, having worked in the company since seventh grade performing a number of menial tasks. After receiving a marketing degree from Millikin University in Decatur, Illinois, Kelly returned to the family business and in 1997 was named vice president and general manager. This move came from a decision by the elder Evans brothers and company employees to bring new and fresh ideas to the company. Tom's son, T. C., has also learned the business from the bottom up, working different tasks during the school years of junior high, high school, and college. A 1993 graduate of the University of Iowa, he joined the family business in 1994 and works as the market support coordinator and continues to be more involved in corporate issues. Dick and his brother Tom continue to be involved in the company as chief executive officer and president respectively.

❖

Above: Evans started as a manufacturer's representative in the bedroom of his home located at 942 West King Street in Decatur, Illinois from 1937 to 1940.

Below: The corporate sales and service center of R. V. Evans Company is located at 2325 East Logan in Decatur, Illinois from 1968 to present.

SAINT XAVIER UNIVERSITY

In 1846, five Sisters of Mercy arrived in the frontier town of Chicago to establish the city's first hospital and found Saint Francis Xavier Female Academy, which today is Saint Xavier University. Chartered in 1847 by the State of Illinois, the academy prepared young women for the world by going beyond lessons in the

domestic arts. Instead, Saint Xavier's former student body gained knowledge across the liberal arts. Years of service and financial prosperity were erased when the Chicago Fire incinerated Saint Xavier in 1871. After the inferno, Saint Xavier would move to Twenty-ninth and Wabash and later, Forty-ninth and Cottage Grove. Saint Xavier Academy became Saint Xavier College for Women in 1915 and established the state's first collegiate nursing program in 1935. In 1956 the college relocated

to 103rd Street and Central Park where the Chicago Campus remains to this day. Saint Xavier became a coeducational institution in 1969 and obtained university status in 1992.

Saint Xavier University now maintains two facilities—the 70-acre Chicago campus, and a 45-acre Orland Park Campus, which opened in 2004. The Chicago Campus comprises academic, administrative, athletic and residential facilities, most of which has been constructed or renovated in the past decade. The university opened the McCarthy and Morris residence halls in 2001 and 2002, respectively. The 85,000-square-foot Shannon Athletic and Convocation Center, built in 1999, features a eighth-mile track, basketball and racquetball courts, Pilates and aerobic workout area and fitness center. In 2000, Saint Xavier added McDonough Chapel, a nondenominational site welcoming students of all backgrounds to practice their faiths.

The university's new Orland Park Campus resulted from a donation of nearly forty-five acres from Robert and Mary Rita Stump, who represent generations of Saint Xavier support. The campus' 31,000-square-foot facility—with 18 classrooms, four computer labs, a cyber cafe, bookstore and library—addresses the need for adult graduate and professional education in Chicago's rapidly growing southwestern suburbs. Bachelor completion and master's programs are offered through the Graham School of Management and School of Education. With its outdoor gardens, the new campus is an educational sanctuary of sorts, situated within a lush wooded wetlands area.

In 2004 the Orland Campus hosted the inaugural session of the Bishop John R. Gorman Institute for Leadership in Catholic Education, inviting Catholic school leaders to grow within their unique field. Maintaining traditions of the founding Sisters of Mercy, Saint Xavier University today continues to promote learning for life and the values of respect, caring and justice.

"I believe in Catholic higher education. I believe it has an important mission in today's culture," said President Judith A. Dwyer, Ph.D., a Catholic moral theologian and author. "It speaks to the transcendence and experience of mystery, which are its hallmarks."

Today Saint Xavier University remains a private, coeducational institution providing more than fifty-seven hundred students with a personalized, high-quality education. Thirty-five bachelor's degrees are offered in four schools: School of Arts and Sciences; Education; Nursing; and the Graham School of Management. The school recently has recorded phenomenal enrollment growth, due in great part to its commitment to provide students with financial aid. More than ninety percent of students receive some kind of financial aid through scholarships, grants, loans and work-study. The university's financial aid office was one of the nation's first to electronically manage all student and institutional information. Since 1998, freshman applications have more than tripled, as Saint Xavier's resident student population has simultaneously posted a similar increase. Meanwhile, graduate student enrollment has increased more than ninety-one percent from 1998 to 2003. The school's student body comprises a wide range of students of all ages, ethnicities and backgrounds. *U.S. News & World Report* has consistently ranked the school as a top college in the Midwest. Saint Xavier was recognized for its commitment to diversity.

Accomplishments continue to be part of Saint Xavier University's rich history. The new Center of International Education, funded by a grant from the United States Department of Education, will enable Saint Xavier to expand its study abroad program and add to the curriculum.

In 2003, Saint Xavier's student-run radio station, WXAV, won five Illinois Broadcasting Association-University Silver Dome awards and recently signed a deal with *USA Network News* to record and produce broadcasts that will be distributed to college radio stations across the country. In the midst of such successes, the university recently completed a strategic planning process, which will inform all aspects of the Saint Xavier's future. "Clearly the focus now will be helping Saint Xavier achieve greater levels of excellence and a higher level of visibility in the greater Chicago metropolitan area and the Midwest," President Dwyer said. "We're already have the foundation, and now we're building on it."

NUDO PRODUCTS, INC.

Imaginative thinking coupled with determination and hard work has established Nudo Products as a leader in the manufacturing of laminate products. It all started in 1954, when, after trying their hands at selling home improvement products door-to-door, Sam Nudo and his brother John opened a retail store, Economy Awning and Tile Company. Eight years later, Sam bought out his brother's interest in the shop, which sold awnings, floor tile, siding, and windows.

After his supplier of fiberglass awnings, Armbruster Manufacturing, decided to stop producing this product, Sam investigated the manufacturing process, acquired the equipment, and was able to realize a lifelong dream of making and selling his own wares. Nudo Products was born when he began to design, manufacture, and sell his own brand of

awnings. Soon his business became the largest fiberglass awning-manufacturing dealer in the entire state of Illinois.

The heavy weight of fiberglass awnings and their resulting high shipping costs limited the company's market area. But in the late 1970s, when Sam was approached about manufacturing specialized lightweight fiberglass panels for the dairy, farming animal confinement buildings and food processing industries, he quickly seized the opportunity.

Laminating fiberglass to plywood panels created the original panels, and Sam quickly realized that this same process could be used to manufacture numerous other products using materials like aluminum, vinyl and plastic. These laminates are bonded to panels of wafer board, particleboard, and plywood, among other materials, and can be single or double sided, with finishes ranging from smooth to texture. They can be made in a variety of patterns and colors; are used in everything from floors to ceilings, walls, signs, countertops, and partitions; and are ideal for restaurants, food processing plants, dog kennels, restrooms, hospitals, and anywhere else durable, sanitary, easy to clean construction materials are needed.

While fiberglass awnings are still made by Nudo, today they make up less than one percent of the products manufactured, marketed and distributed nationally and internationally by the company. Sam gives a lot of credit for the firm's expansion to his sons, and in fact his entire family has been involved with Nudo Products. His wife, Wanda, raised their five sons and then later became president of the company. All of the boys have worked for the company at one time or another. Today, Sam Jr., Tim, and Pat are the main partners in the business, while Sam Sr., describes himself as one of their employees.

The laminating process led the company to manufacture pieces to join and finish their panels using a profile extrusion process. Plastic profile pieces, moldings, corners, caps and more are created in this process, which turns vinyl or plastic pellets into a liquid that is forced continuously through a die, creating the desired shaped piece.

When the company could not find the quality materials needed to install its products, it became self-supporting, crafting all of its own materials. It began using an injection molding system to manufacture rivets, screws and other fasteners which will not rust, rot, peel, or corrode and are used to attach panels to wood, brick, stone, concrete, and other substrates. One of its latest manufacturing processes is sheet extrusion, which allows Nudo Products to create its own laminating materials. It employs a continuous flow of plastic or vinyl material that produces sheets in rolls up to 60 inches wide and weighing up to 1,000 pounds.

There is a constant stream of new product lines and capabilities at Nudo and an additional building space or product line has been added almost every year since 1990. Its latest product is Nu-Ice, a synthetic ice skating surface that requires no water or refrigeration.

A new treatment process that applies a durable plastic coating to routed edges has been recently introduced, in addition to heat laminating equipment that reduces curing times and adds flexibility in the production of composite core products. The company also boasts its own machining capabilities, allowing the creation of tongue and groove panels and making it possible to cut and route shapes for counters and tabletops.

While these new lines keep the company vibrant, its focus is still kept on producing top quality goods at competitive prices. Throughout the years the firm has earned their fine repu-tation by offering a wide range of manufacturing capabilities, terrific

customer service and support and an excellent distribution system.

Nudo Products has grown enormously, and today has over 150 employees working out of several buildings in a two city-block area in Springfield. It produces thousands of various panels every day, holds several patents, and offers registered and trademarked products including Fiber-Lite, Nu-Poly, Nu-Alum, and FiberCorr. Using the same imaginative thinking that brought the Nudo family such success over the past fifty years, the company will continue to streamline and improve its manufacturing processes and create new products well into the future.

For more information about Nudo Products, Inc., please visit www.nudo.com.

✧

Above: The Nudo Products family. Back row (from left to right): Denies Nudo, Bob Carr, Carrell Miller, Wanda Nudo, Samuel Nudo, Sr., Lenny Long, Jimmy Elliott, John Bednarko, Emo Wisner, and DeWayne Beard. Front row: Tom Nudo, Pat Nudo, Samuel Nudo, Jr., and Tim Nudo.

WILLIAMS-MANNY INC.

BY ANNA HART

The largest independent insurance agency in northern Illinois, Williams-Manny has provided insurance protection for over a century, including a wide range of commercial property/casualty, personal lines, employee benefits, individual life and health coverage, plus risk management services.

Henry "Hank" Williams, an affable, energetic man, was the company's founder and proprietor until his death in 1945. An avid photographer, he captured one of the best fire shots of the era—of Rockford's Second Congregational Church as flames leaped through its upper floor windows in 1894. He was paid $25 by the *Chicago Tribune* for two prints and an accompanying story; and an illustration of the photograph appeared on his agency's letterhead for fifty years.

Williams began his insurance career as an employee of the Rockford Fire Insurance Company. In 1896, at age twenty-five, he launched his own firm, initially using his mother's sewing machine stand as a desk. His first contract was with the Germania Fire Insurance Company, and within six years he represented more than three dozen insurers. The enterprising young agent would follow passing lumber trucks, find out who was building a house or factory...and then write the insurance on it.

His volume of work increasing, Williams hired Frank Wormwood as solicitor, and then partner. In 1913, Williams asked banking professional Dwight Manny to join the firm. He wrote: "We have by far the best chance of any firm in Rockford if we will only work hard and be square with ourselves and everyone we do business for."

The values expressed in that letter of trust, honesty, and diligence have continued to be the hallmarks of Williams-Manny through the years:

- In 1913 the firm was named the Williams-Manny Company. (Dwight Manny was the grandson of John P. Manny, inventor of the reaper who prevailed, with Abraham Lincoln as associate counsel, in a patent infringement suit brought by Cyrus McCormick.)
- In 1922, Victor Engstrom, whose father T. Victor Engstrom founded the Forest City Insurance Company, joined the firm.
- In 1931 the name was changed to Williams, Manny, Stevens & Engstrom when Webb C. Stevens, lawyer, retired co-founder of Keig-Stevens Baking Company and civic leader, came on board.
- In 1968 the agency name was changed to Williams-Manny, Inc.
  Subsequently, the firm:
- Added engineering staff as a core area of expertise (from the 1930s to the 1960s, Rockford was a major furniture manufacturing center in the Midwest);
- Moved to its Perryville Road location (1989);
- Merged with local agency, Herrling & Schmitt, Inc (1997);
- Received the inaugural "Agency of the Year" award by the Professional Independent Insurance Agents of Illinois (2002);
- Was named a "Best Practices" agency by the Independent Insurance Agents & Brokers of America (2004).

For more information on Williams-Manny Inc., please visit www.williamsmanny.com.

✧

Right: Visionary Henry W. "Hank" Williams (1871-1945).

Below: Hank Williams' award-winning photo of the Second Congregational Church of Rockford on fire, taken February 20, 1894.

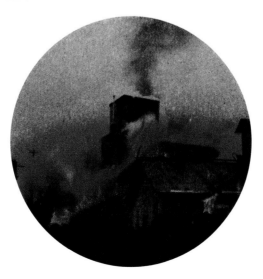

Located on the border between Kankakee and Iroquois Counties, Chebanse Ag Service has been serving the needs of area farmers for over thirty years. The owners and employees of the company have sought to meet the needs of customers in an equitable and timely manner while providing the best service possible. Chebanse's principal owners, the Schafer family, have deep roots in the community, which go back much further than the founding of the company.

In 1867, Anton Schafer purchased a 160-acre tract of land located in Chebanse Township in Iroquois County. Proving to be a successful farmer, Anton added several more acres to his holdings before his retirement in 1891. He instilled in his children a love for farming that has been passed down to the present generation of the Schafer family. Five generations of Schafers have tilled this farm and added to its acreage down to the current owner, Donald Schafer, who continues to follow in the steps of his ancestors.

In addition to farming, Donald Schafer began selling nitrogen and fertilizer to fellow farmers in 1963. He and his wife, Elsie, continued to develop the business, in addition to a busy farming schedule. When his sons David and Dennis became old enough to handle the farming operations on their own, Don turned his full attention to the fertilizer business. He incorporated Chebanse Crop Service in 1970 with a formal structure of stockholders who advise on expansion and development. Property was leased in Chebanse, Illinois, and the fertilizer business continued on a larger scale. The company now sells and applies fertilizer, nitrogen and chemicals as well as providing consultation on crop production.

The Schafers expanded their business by purchasing the Chebanse Elevator in 1976, establishing Chebanse Grain & Lumber.

Storage and railroad facilities have been improved by relocating the business to a site north of town with the aim of keeping costs down for customers. Several other elevator purchases followed; presently the company has facilities in Greenwich, Papineau, Irwin, Beaverville, and Elwood, Illinois.

Chebanse Ag Service and Chebanse Grain continue to be family owned and operated businesses. Don Schafer is officially retired but remains active by assisting farmers with their concerns. Don's son, Dean, daughter Ann and son-in-law, Keith Jensen have assumed management of the company with Don acting as consultant. Many of the employees have been with the company for many years giving the customers a good feeling of continuity.

Under Don's management Chebanse Ag Service and Chebanse Grain have flourished. With the next generation's guidance, the companies will continue to provide products and service to farmers at a fair marketable price and remain a friend to the agricultural community.

❖

Above: An aerial photograph of Chebanse Ag & Grain, c. 1998.
COURTESY OF MIDWEST PHOTOGRAPHY.

Below: The homestead as it appears today.

CHEBANSE AG SERVICE

CHEBANSE GRAIN

KENNICOTT BROTHERS

For over 100 years Kennicott Brothers has been a growing business. Founded in 1881 by Amasa and Flint Kennicott in Chicago, this company was the first wholesale florist in the Midwest. Today Kennicott Brothers is a major importer of flowers from all over the world and distributor to retail florists, wholesale florists and supermarkets across the United States.

Kennicott Brothers' beginning took root in 1836 when Dr. John A. Kennicott, father of Amasa and Flint, founded The Grove Nursery on land purchased from the federal government located on the Milwaukee Stage Road in Northfield Township near what is now Glenview. Dr. Kennicott was successful as a horticulturalist and his nursery thrived. By the 1840s he was selling rose bushes and other nursery products in the Chicago market. An avid promoter of agriculture, Dr. Kennicott was an early editor of the *Prairie Farmer*, Illinois' oldest farm magazine. He was also involved in the establishment of the United States Department of Agriculture and passage of the Morrill Act, which established Land Grant Colleges.

Amasa and Flint Kennicott established their firm in 1881 to market the fresh flower production of The Grove Nursery. They opened for business on Wabash Avenue in Chicago. The City of Chicago blossomed as a major center of flower production during the late 1800s with its dominance as a railroad hub. By the early 1900s Chicago was home to more than thirty wholesalers and hundreds of growers. Kennicott Brothers thrived and became a leading shipper of flowers throughout the central and southern parts of the United States.

Kennicott Brothers remained a family business with the addition of H. B. "Hal" Kennicott, son of Flint, who served as president of the company from 1915 to 1972. His nephew, Harrison Kennicott, Jr., grandson of Amasa, joined the company in 1929 and led the company from the 1940s until his retirement in 1980. The company flourished under his direction, especially in the years following the World War II. Branch locations were opened in Waukegan (1963), Aurora (1965), Hammond, Indiana (1970), Milwaukee, Wisconsin (1975) and Elk Grove (2000). Harrison "Red" Kennicott is the present CEO of the company. Kennicott Brothers, currently located at 452 North Ashland Avenue, employs over 200 people and serves a customer base of over 2000 floral retailers. In 2000 the company became 100 percent employee owned with the Kennicott Family remaining active in floral production.

From its initial days as The Grove Nursery to its present role as a leading distributor of fresh flowers and related products, Kennicott Brothers has had its astounding success by placing customers first.

Levi, Ray & Shoup, Inc., one of the Springfield area's most phenomenal success stories, has a history of technological excellence and innovation. Founded by three friends in 1979, LRS has grown to become a global provider of innovative information technology solutions with more than 550 employees. From corporate headquarters in Springfield, LRS operates six offices in the United States and five more around the globe: Madrid, Spain; Frankfort and Munich, Germany; Cheltenham, England; and Sydney, Australia. A network of 13 international distributors also markets LRS software, which is used by a majority of *Fortune 500* firms and in more than 30 countries around the world. The company is ranked by *Software Magazine* as one of the top two hundred software companies in the world.

When they founded LRS in 1979, partners Dick Levi, Roger Ray and Bob Shoup specialized in providing consulting services to a variety of local companies and state agencies. Ray and Shoup eventually sold their share to Dick Levi. As the company matured, it developed products and services in specific information technology areas.

In 1981 LRS developed the first software that enabled MVS mainframe systems to distribute output to printers outside the data center. Today LRS leads the industry in Enterprise Output Management products, and its core product, VTAM Printer Support (VPS®), runs on more than five thousand mainframes worldwide.

LRS IT Solutions continues the LRS consulting tradition, providing custom application

development, hardware, networking, and software consulting services. An IBM Premier Business Partner, LRS IT Solutions operates one of only sixty IBM TotalStorage Solution Centers in the U.S. and sells a variety of computer hardware. Microsoft Gold Certified Partner status also recognizes our consulting expertise.

LRS PensionGold software helps pension plan administrators automate data tracking and administrative tasks to increase productivity and member satisfaction.

LRS Education Services, certified by Microsoft and Novell, provides networking, network management, and productivity software training to organizations and individuals.

LRSSports Software Systems offers products focusing on the full range of needs of athletic programs at the high school, collegiate, and professional levels.

LRS Web Services offers clients complete Web site services from creative design through site layout, page building, and custom business applications.

Information Services provides data processing services for numerous clients.

Today LRS fills an impressive office complex on West Monroe. But the company's commitment to the community is more than buildings; it is also financial support and participation in civic projects, charities and nonprofit groups. LRS sponsors local NHRA funny car driver Tim Wilkerson and is a major sponsor of the annual LPGA State Farm Classic golf tournament.

An international firm dedicated to advancing technology, LRS serves its clients and our community with distinction.

LEVI, RAY & SHOUP, INC.

❖

Above: The Levi, Ray & Shoup, Inc., offices in Springfield, Illinois.

Below: The lobby of the Levi, Ray & Shoup, Inc., offices.

SOLOMON
COLORS

Founded in 1927 by Robert C. Solomon, for over seventy-five years Springfield-based Solomon Colors has produced high quality pigments for the construction industry. Robert C. Solomon's father was orphaned during the Civil War and went to work as a coalminer at thirteen, later operating mines with his sons. Following in his dad's footsteps, by 1927 Robert C. was the operator at the Panther Creek Coal Mine. The Solomon Grinding Company was born after he hit on the idea of pulverizing a mining byproduct, black carbonaceous slate, to create pigments to color mortar and cement.

Initially the company was involved in the underground mining of coal as well as the crushing, grinding, and blending of various natural minerals, including red iron ore from Michigan and yellow ochre from Georgia. Several years later, as area coalmining was phased out, the business shifted direction and began providing various grind levels of iron ore to the foundry and trace mineral industries.

Robert C.'s wife and business partner, Florence Larson Solomon, took over the company after he died in 1959. Their son, Robert L., assumed the helm of Solomon Colors in the early 1960s.

As synthetic iron oxide pigments became the firm's mainstay, the business changed its name to Solomon Colors. At this juncture, the Solomons decided it was time to package their pigments under their own name, instead of just selling its products to other pigment companies, as they had done for nearly fifty years. But because the company didn't have the financial resources to start this new venture in 1972, Robert L. sold his home and used the proceeds to get the business up and running.

Fortunately, Solomon Colors products were a success from the start, largely due to the company's outstanding employees, both past and present. The Solomon family believes that their employees have made the firm what is today and instituted an employee stock option plan, which today has made the business thirty percent employee-owned. The family legacy started by Robert C., is still going strong with his son, Robert L., serving as CEO, and grandson Richard R. Solomon, who's been with the company since finishing college in 1979, serving as president.

The firm now has over 130 employees working in two plants in Springfield, Illinois, and Rialto, California, as well as a crew of salesman operating around the country. It is the largest American-owned producer of iron oxide pigments and is looked to by contractors across the U.S. for the finest pigments to add value and visual appeal to mortar, pavers, roof tile, stucco, grout, concrete brick, and other precast products. Solomon produces both dry and liquid pigments for ready-mix and concrete applications and has revolutionized the industry with its exclusive ColorSelect Liquid Dispensing System.

For more information about Solomon Colors, please visit www.solomoncolors.com.

❖

Above: Robert C. Solomon founded Solomon Grinding Service in 1927 while he was operator of the Panther Creek Coal Mines.

Below: (left) Richard R. Solomon, president and Robert L. Solomon, CEO (right) proudly display a pallet of 25-pound ready mix color bags, 4,000-pound Colorflo™ liquid tote, and a pallet of concentrated mortar color cases.

ILLINOIS STATE HISTORICAL SOCIETY

BY WILLIAM FURRY

Exploring and preserving Prairie State history since 1899, the Illinois State Historical Society, a not-for-profit organization with headquarters in Springfield, the state capital, was established in 1899 to foster awareness, understanding, research, preservation, and recognition of Illinois history. Chartered in 1900 and by action of the Illinois General Assembly made a support arm for the Illinois State Historical Library in 1903, the Society is the leading advocate for the preservation and promotion of the Prairie State's past.

Today the Society operates independently of the State Historical Library (now Abraham Lincoln Presidential Library) and its umbrella agency, the Illinois Historic Preservation Agency, receiving no government funding for its various programs and publications. The Society relies solely upon membership dues, program receipts, publication sales, investments, fundraising, and member bequests to fulfill its mission.

Society programs include: Historical Markers, which recognize historic events, people, and places in the state; the Centennial Awards, which commemorate Illinois businesses and organizations that have operated for one hundred years or more; the Illinois History Symposium, which promotes and provides an audience for the latest historical research in the state; and the Annual Meeting, which brings the Society membership together for tours and celebrations of our unique heritage. The Society also publishes *The Journal of the Illinois State Historical Society*, the quarterly journal of record featuring the latest historical scholarship; and *Illinois Heritage*, a bimonthly popular history magazine.

The Society's organizational structure includes a Board of Directors and Advisory Board, which consist of professional and amateur historians, teachers, lawyers, museum curators, archivists, and civic leaders from all over Illinois. Its membership includes citizens from all walks of life, as well as libraries, historical societies, museums, public and private corporations, and small businesses.

The Illinois State Historical Society welcomes participation at all levels and encourages you to share your Illinois heritage with others. Become a member. For more information about the Society, call 217-525-2781, or visit us on the Internet at www.historyillinois.org.

✧

Top: Abraham Lincoln, photo by Alexander Hesler, taken June 3, 1860, in Springfield, Illinois. From the collection of the Illinois State Historical Society.

Above: William Furry, executive director of the Illinois State Historical Society.

INDEX